Basic Grammar and Usage for Canadians

Second Edition

Penelope Choy
Los Angeles City College

Dorothy Goldbart Clark
California State University, Northridge

Shirley Turchet
Seneca College, Faculty of Continuing Education

THOMSON
━━━✷━━━ ™
NELSON

Australia   Canada   Mexico   Singapore   Spain   United Kingdom   United States

THOMSON
★
NELSON™

Basic Grammar and Usage for Canadians
Second Edition

by Penelope Choy, Dorothy Goldbart Clark, and Shirley Turchet

Associate Vice President, Editorial Director:
Evelyn Veitch

Editor-in-Chief, Higher Education:
Anne Williams

Executive Editor:
Laura Macleod

Marketing Manager:
Sandra Green

Developmental Editor:
Beth Lariviere

Senior Content Production Manager:
Julie van Veen

Copy Editor:
Wayne Herrington

Proofreader:
Gail Marsden

Indexer:
Elizabeth Bell

Production Coordinator:
Ferial Suleman

Design Director:
Ken Phipps

Interior Design Modifications:
Jack Steiner

Cover Design:
Johanna Liburd
Peter Papayanakis

Compositor:
Nelson Gonzalez

Printer:
Thomson West

Library and Archives Canada Cataloguing in Publication Data

Choy, Penelope
   Basic grammar and usage for Canadians / Penelope Choy, Dorothy Goldbart Clark, Shirley Turchet.—2nd ed.

First Canadian ed. published under title: Grammar and usage.
Includes index.
ISBN-13: 978-0-17-610336-1
ISBN-10: 0-17-610336-8

1. English language—Grammar. I. Clark, Dorothy Goldbart II. Turchet, Shirley, 1946– III. Choy, Penelope Grammar and usage. Title.

PE1112.C48 2007   428.2
C2006-903635-7

CONTENTS

PREFACE

More than twenty-five years have passed since the 1978 publication of the first edition of *Basic Grammar and Usage* in the United States. As in previous revisions, this edition includes new exercises for each chapter, and the Instructor's Manual has new tests.

Also new to this edition is a chapter on composing paragraphs, written by Dorothy Clark. This chapter presents writing effective paragraphs as a key to opening the world of academic writing, a world the authors realize can be challenging to many students. Following the organizational principles of the rest of *Basic Grammar and Usage,* the chapter moves from simple to more complex activities: from understanding what a paragraph is (for example, dividing blocks of text into separate paragraphs and identifying and constructing topic sentences) to studying the paragraph's controlling principles, such as unity and coherence, to reviewing specific organizational strategies. Each section of the chapter has many examples of good and bad paragraph writing, and exercises are included for all the sections.

Additional changes have been made at the suggestion of reviewers, such as a clarification of ways to avoid sexist language, an updating of the distinction between *which* and *that* in adjective clauses, and a change in the exercises provided for irregular verbs. However, the basic organization of the text, which has accounted for its continued use over a four-decade period, remains unchanged.

Basic Grammar and Usage for Canadians begins with a unit on identifying subjects and verbs, which provides a foundation for the rest of the book. It continues with five other units, each devoted to a specific area of grammar, such as subject–verb agreement. Each unit is divided into four or five chapters to make acquisition of the information easier for the students. For example, the subject–verb agreement unit has one chapter focusing on indefinite pronoun subjects (including the rules for quantifiers, such as *most* and *some*). A separate chapter deals with compound subjects joined by conjunctions like *and* or *or.* Each chapter includes clear explanations of grammar rules and structures and provides copious examples for each point. Short exercises for each new grammar point occur throughout every chapter.

At the end of each chapter are two longer exercises. Exercise A covers the material presented in that particular chapter. Exercise B reviews material covered in earlier chapters in the unit to ensure that students remember what they have previously studied and are able to see the relationships among the various chapters. For example, in Chapter 13, students learn to recognize and to punctuate parenthetical expressions. In Chapter 14, they are introduced to appositives, which are punctuated in the same way. Having mastered appositives, the students move on in Chapter 15 to restrictive and nonrestrictive adjective clauses. This usually challenging topic is made easier because the students now see the adjective clause as simply an expansion of the information contained in an appositive, and they already know the punctuation rules for separating "extra" information from the rest of the sentence. To help in holding the students' interest, most of the "A" and "B" exercises are written in narrative form on a wide variety of topics. A comprehensive review at the end of each unit tests the students' knowledge of the entire sequence of lessons for that unit. All the exercises and unit reviews are on perforated pages that the students can remove from the book. Answers to the "A" exercises are printed in the appendix so that students can check their own work. Answers to the "B" exercises are printed in the Instructor's Manual, which is described in more detail below.

Throughout these exercises, we have tried to go beyond simple fill-in-the-blank and choose-the-correct-answer items and have emphasized recognizing and correcting errors. A typical chapter first has students identify which numbered items in an "A" exercise contain a specific error, such as a run-on sentence or a comma splice. The "B" exercise for the chapter is a multiparagraph essay in which students must identify and correct errors within the context of an entire page of prose. This emphasis on error correction reflects our belief that the primary reason for studying grammar and usage is to help students learn to correct these errors in their own writing and, ultimately, to avoid making these mistakes in the future.

An Instructor's Manual is available to anyone who adopts this book. Besides the answers to the "B" exercises, the manual contains detailed unit tests to supplement the unit reviews that are included in the text. Brief, but comprehensive, diagnostic tests for each unit are also provided so that instructors who do not plan to use the entire book can determine which units their students need to study. Achievement tests, which are identical in format to the diagnostic tests, measure what the students have learned after completing the course. (By "identical in format," we mean that item number one on the diagnostic test for Unit 1 covers the same grammar rule as item number one on the achievement test.) We suggest that the diagnostic tests be given at the beginning of the semester and that the achievement tests be given at the end of the course. If instructors prefer to use their own tests, these exams may be used for extra practice. The tests are printed on 8.5- by 11-inch loose-leaf pages for convenient reproduction, and answers for each exam are included in the Instructor's Manual.

Although *Basic Grammar and Usage* was originally designed for students whose first language is English, it has been used successfully by students learning English as a second language. In addition to being a classroom text, *Basic Grammar and Usage* can also be used in writing labs and for individual study.

ABOUT THE CANADIAN EDITION

The Second Edition of Choy and Clark's *Basic Grammar and Usage* presents all the revisions and strengths of the American Thomson Wadsworth's Seventh Edition, noteworthy for its developmental organization and user-friendly, context-driven exercises.

Capitalizing on the many pedagogically sound changes made at reviewers' suggestions in the American editions, the Second Edition presents material that reflects Canada's national and regional diversity in the Canadian historical, political, geographical, and social references. It also uses preferred Canadian spellings, metric measurements, and Canadian usage to give a more relevant context that supports integration of the material with students' prior knowledge. In addition, this text uses personal names more reflective of our multicultural identity to encourage student engagement. Useful summary information from the American Edition has been included on the inside front and back covers, reorganized under function headings and expanded to include additional verb information and tenses, for students' quick reference.

The U.S. prefaces have been retained, as they clearly outline the changes made to previous editions and explain the text's developmental organization and user assists.

▶ Where an arrow appears in the margin, students are to follow the instructions given.

An instructor's manual (ISBN 0-17-610530-1) is provided to instructors who teach from the text. The instructor's manual contains all the answers to the "B" exercises. The "B" exercises are cumulative for the entire unit. Many of the "B" exercises involve proofreading and correction of errors.

ACKNOWLEDGMENTS

Many people have participated in the preparation of this book. We are grateful to the instructors who reviewed our text and suggested revisions for the current edition:

Margaret Amman, *University of Alaska at Anchorage*
Susan Bury, *University of Alaska at Anchorage*
James Davis, *University of Alaska at Anchorage*
Debra Jones, *Albany Technical College*
Michael Kent, *Riverside Community College*
Nita Kincaid, *Los Angeles City College*
Carole Martin, *Southwest Minnesota State University*
Ann Spicer, *Wayne Community College*
Laura Wheeler, *Long Beach Community College*

We would like to thank our developmental editor, Cathy Dodson; our production manager at Thomson Wadsworth, Karen Stocz; the project manager at Cadmus, M.R. Carey; and the composition manager at Cadmus, Mary Dissinger, for seeing the book into print.

Penelope Choy would like to thank her stepson and computer expert, Joel Rothman, for the many hours he spent preparing the manuscript for this edition. This project could not have been completed without him. She would also like to thank her husband, Gene Rothman, for his endless patience and good humor during the months she was preoccupied with her work on this book.

Dorothy Clark would like to thank her husband, Kevin O'Neill, for his constant loving support and creative encouragement; her children, Ben and Julia, for the inspiration they offer; and her students, for the lessons they continue to teach her.

We would both like to thank the many instructors and the thousands of students who have used our book during the past four decades. Both of us are still teaching composition courses and encountering students with little or no knowledge of grammar and usage. We know personally the relief those students feel when they realize that English grammar is comprehensible and systematic. We hope that your students have similarly successful experiences.

Penelope Choy
Dorothy Goldbart Clark

I would like to acknowledge the many people involved in the production of this book, including the instructors who reviewed the American Seventh Edition and made suggestions for the revisions of this edition: Rhonda Schuller, University College of the Fraser Valley; and Martha Finnigan, School of Business, Durham College.

Many thanks go to the Thomson Nelson publishing team of Anne Williams, Editor-in-Chief; Lenore Spence, Director, Development; Beth Lariviere, Developmental Editor; Susan Calvert, Director of Content Production; Julie van Veen, Senior Content Production Manager; Wayne Herrington, copy editor; and Gail Marsden, proofreader.

I would also like to note the assistance provided by my husband Mario, daughter Daniella, and son Stefan in bringing me into the 21st century to work online.

I would be remiss if I didn't thank my college students for helping me, and all instructors, learn what is most useful to them, and how to assist them to master and build on "the basics" as they grapple with the challenge of clear and meaningful written expression in today's electronic age.

Many thanks go to the instructors who use this book, as part of the class session or assigned for individual review and practice. I hope it makes your teaching more manageable and productive.

And last, but most significantly, a big thank-you to the students who use this text; may it demystify grammar for you and help you become more successful communicators.

Shirley Turchet
Seneca College, Faculty of Continuing Education
Toronto, Ontario

Unit

1

Identifying Subjects and Verbs

Chapter 1

Sentences with One Subject and One Verb

The most important grammatical skill you can learn is how to identify subjects and verbs. Just as solving arithmetic problems requires that you know the multiplication tables perfectly, solving grammatical problems requires you to identify subjects and verbs with perfect accuracy. This is not as difficult as it may sound. With practice, recognizing subjects and verbs will become as automatic as knowing that $2 + 2 = 4$.

Although in conversation people often speak in short word groups that may not be complete sentences, in writing it is customary to use complete sentences.

A complete sentence contains at least one subject and one verb.

A sentence can be thought of as a statement describing an *actor* performing a particular *action*. For example, in the sentence "The dog ran," the *actor* or person performing the action is the dog. What *action* did the dog perform? He *ran*. This *actor–action* pattern can be found in most sentences. Can you identify the actor and the action in each of the following sentences?

The teacher laughed.
The crowd applauded.

The actor in a sentence is called the **subject.** The action word in a sentence is called the **verb.** Together, the subject and the verb form the core of the sentence. Notice that even if extra words are added to the two sentences above, the subject–verb core in each sentence remains the same.

The teacher laughed at the student's joke.
After the performance, the crowd applauded enthusiastically.

You can see that to identify subjects and verbs, you must be able to separate these core words from the rest of the words in the sentence.
Here are some suggestions to help you identify verbs.

1. The *action* words in sentences are verbs. For example,

The team *played* well.
This store *sells* rare books.
The doctor *recommended* vitamins.

► Underline the verb in each of the following sentences.

The bank lends money to small businesses.
Gina speaks Italian.
The flood destroyed many homes.

2. All forms of the verb "to be" are verbs: *am, is, are, was, were,* and *been.* For example,

Susan *is* unhappy.
The actor *was* nervous.

Verbs also include words that can be used as substitutes for forms of *be,* such as *seem, feel, become,* and *appear.* These verbs are called **linking** or **auxiliary verbs.**

Susan *seems* unhappy.
The actor *appeared* nervous.

▶ Underline the verb in each of the following sentences.

The children became excited during the birthday party.

The professor seemed fatigued today.

The actors felt happy with their performances.

3. Verbs are the only words that change their spelling to show tense. **Tense** is the time—present, past, or future—at which the verb's action occurs. For example, the sentence "We *walk* each morning" has a present-tense verb.
▶ The sentence "We *walked* each morning" has a past-tense verb. Underline the verb in each of the following sentences.

Grandfather moves today.

My brother moved to Edmonton last month.

Tanjima dances very well.

Maria danced on her wedding day.

I wash my hair every morning.

The nurse washed her hands.

Identifying verbs will be easier for you if you remember that the following kinds of words are *not* verbs.

4. An **infinitive**—the combination of the word *to* plus a verb, such as *to walk* or *to study*—is not considered part of the verb in a sentence. Read the following sentences.

He plans to swim later.

She wants to enter graduate school.

The main verbs in these two sentences are *plans* and *wants*. The infinitives
▶ *to swim* and *to enter* are not included. Underline the main verb in each of the following sentences.

Benjy decided to play his new video games.

The conductor promised to check our luggage.

5. **Adverbs**—words that describe a verb—are *not* part of the verb. Many commonly used adverbs end in *-ly*. The adverbs in the following sentences
▶ are italicized. Underline the verb in each sentence.

The guitarist played *badly.*

Phillipe rushed *quickly* to our rescue.

The mother *patiently* helped her children.

▶ The words *not, never,* and *very* are also adverbs. Like other adverbs, these words are not part of the verb. Underline the verb in each of the following sentences. Do *not* include adverbs.

The dancers are not here yet.

He never studies for his tests.

The director spoke very carefully.

He is not a good mechanic.

Mario never remembers to close the door.

Now that you can identify verbs, here are some suggestions to help you identify subjects.

▶ 1. The subject of a sentence is most often a noun. A **noun** is the name of a person, place, or thing, such as *Julia, Montreal,* or *pens.* A noun may also be the name of an abstract idea, such as *sadness* or *failure.* Underline the subject in each of the following sentences *once* and the verb *twice.* Remember that the verb is the *action,* and the subject is the *actor.*

Kevin reads many books each month.

The store closes at midnight.

Athens hosted the 2004 Summer Olympics.

Love conquers all.

2. The subject of a sentence may also be a **subject pronoun.** A **pronoun** is a word used in place of a noun, such as *she* (= *Julia*), *it* (= *Montreal*), or *they* (= *pens*). The following words are subject pronouns:

I, you, he, she, it, we, they

▶ Underline the subject in each of the following sentences *once* and the verb *twice.*

He was Prime Minister of Canada.

Each spring they travel to Banff National Park.

I always drink strong coffee.

We rarely have dinner out on weekdays.

You washed the dishes last night.

3. The subject of a sentence may also be a **gerund**. A **gerund** is an *-ing* form of a verb used as a noun. For example, in the sentence "Swimming is an excellent form of exercise," the subject of the sentence is the gerund *swimming*. ▶ Underline the gerund subjects in the following sentences *once* and the verbs *twice*.

Listening is difficult for young children.

Dieting makes me very hungry.

4. In **commands** (also known as **imperatives**)—such as "Wash the dishes!"— the subject is understood to be the subject pronoun *you* even though the word *you* is almost never included in the command. *You* is understood to be the subject of the following sentences:

Do your homework early.

Consider the alternative.

▶ Underline the subject in each of the following sentences *once* and the verb *twice*. If the sentence is a command, write the subject *you* in parentheses at the beginning of the sentence.

Remember to wipe your feet before entering.

The judge reviewed the verdict.

They bowl every Wednesday.

Discuss these issues with your colleagues.

Identifying subjects will be easier for you if you remember that the following kinds of words are *not* subjects.

5. **Adjectives**—words that describe a noun—are *not* part of the subject. For example, in the sentence "The tall boy runs well," the subject is "boy," *not* "tall boy." In the sentence "A new car is a great joy," the subject is "car," ▶ *not* "new car." Underline the subject in each of the following sentences *once* and the verb *twice*.

A talented singer performed that song.

Chocolate cake is his favourite food.

Small pets delight our family.

An angry, bitter debate ended the program.

6. Words that show **possession,** or ownership, are *not* part of the subject. Words that show possession include nouns ending in an apostrophe (') combined with *s*, such as *Dina's* or *cat's*. They also include **possessive pronouns,** words that replace nouns showing ownership, such as *hers* (= *Dina's*) or *its* (= *cat's*). Possessive pronouns include the following words:

mine, yours, his, hers, its, ours, theirs. (**Possessive adjectives** include my, your, his, her, its, their.)

Because words that show possession are *not* part of the subject, in the sentence "My dog has fleas," the subject is "dog," *not* "my dog." In the sentence "Sarah's mother is a doctor," the subject is "mother," *not* "Sarah's mother."

▶ Underline the subject in each of the following sentences *once* and the verb *twice*.

His daughter became a doctor.

My brother works in another city.

This beach's beauty is startling.

Harry's car needs a new battery.

Here is a final suggestion to help you identify subjects and verbs accurately.

Try to identify the verb in a sentence before you try to identify the subject.

A sentence may have many nouns, any of which could be the subject, but it will usually have only one or two verbs. For example,

The director of the play shouted angry words to all the actors and staff.

There are five nouns in the above sentence (*director, play, words, actors, staff*), any of which might be the subject. However, there is only one verb—*shouted*. Once you have identified the verb as *shouted,* all you have to ask yourself is, "Who or what shouted?" The answer is *director,* which is the subject of the sentence.

▶ Identify the subject and verb in the following sentence, remembering to look for the verb first.

In the winter, our family travels to the mountains for our vacation.

Remember these basic points:

1. The action being performed in a sentence is the **verb.**
2. The person or thing performing the action is the **subject.**
3. A sentence consists of an *actor* performing an *action,* or, in other words, a **subject** plus a **verb.**

Every sentence you write will have a subject and a verb, so you must be able to identify subjects and verbs to write correctly. Therefore, as you do the exercises in this unit, apply the rules you have learned in each lesson, and think about what you are doing. Do not make random guesses. Grammar is based on logic, not on luck.

▶ Underline the subject in each of the following sentences *once* and the verb *twice.* Add the subject *you* in parentheses if the sentence is a command.

That man won the contest yesterday.

Success makes us happy.

The ancient horse slowly pulled the cart.

Wisdom is endless.

Consider the virtues of discipline.

My little sister's dance recital was lots of fun.

A quiet garden is my favourite place to read.

Your family's last vacation sounds very exciting.

EXERCISE 1A

▶ Underline the subject of each sentence *once* and the verb *twice*. Each sentence has one subject and one verb. *Remember to look for the verb first* before you try to locate the subject.

1. Chocolate is a favourite food of many people.

2. It comes from the seeds of the cacao tree.

3. Most people call these pods "cocoa beans."

4. Europeans never tasted chocolate until the early 16th century.

5. Then, in 1519, Spanish conquerors found chocolate in Mexico.

6. The Aztecs in Mexico crushed their cocoa beans to make a cold beverage.

7. Hernan Cortez brought chocolate from Mexico to Spain in 1528.

8. The Spaniards used sugar and hot water in their version of the beverage.

9. From Spain, chocolate gradually spread throughout the rest of Europe.

10. By the mid-1600s, drinking cocoa was a popular pastime.

11. The public even gathered in "chocolate houses" to enjoy the new beverage.

12. Chocolate's reputation as a cure for hangovers was partly responsible for its popularity.

13. Chocolate existed only as a beverage until the 1720s.

14. Then, in 1728, the first chocolate candy appeared.

15. The most famous name in the Canadian chocolate industry is Laura Secord.

16. Laura Secord was a Canadian heroine in the War of 1812.

17. Laura Secord trekked 32 kilometres through the forest to warn the British army of an American ambush.

18. One hundred years later, a chocolate maker named his new shop after Laura Secord to commemorate the anniversary of her mission.

19. The average Canadian purchases 6.7 kilograms of chocolate each year as candy and other chocolate products.

20. Eating chocolate possibly has some health benefits.

21. Dark chocolate contains more antioxidants than either green or black tea.

22. Another substance in chocolate seems to lower the risk of heart disease.

23. Finally, some chocolate components improve people's moods.

24. They act like natural antidepressants.

EXERCISE 1B

▶ Underline the subject of each sentence *once* and the verb *twice*. Each sentence has one subject and one verb. *Remember to look for the verb first* before you try to locate the subject.

1. Poetry seems old-fashioned or dull to some people.

2. Poetry slams completely changed that idea.

3. They are exciting, interactive events.

4. Poets come to perform their poetry in a theatrical fashion.

5. The audience comes to judge both the poetry and the poets' performances.

6. Any person is free to sign up to perform a poem.

7. An emcee chooses judges from the audience.

8. Each poet then performs for no longer than three minutes.

9. The format allows the audience to react to the poet's performance, the judges' scores, and the emcee's banter.

10. The audience shows its opinion by cheering, booing, foot stomping, and finger snapping.

11. Poetry slams began at Chicago's Green Mill Tavern in 1986.

12. Marc Smith created the Uptown Poetry Slam to breathe new life into poetry.

13. Smith's goal was to establish a vibrant community of poets and poetry-loving people.

14. Poetry slams present a different kind of poem than traditional poetry.

15. Its practitioners use the phrase "spoken word" to describe it.

16. These poets believe strongly in poetry's oral value.

17. A poem for them is much more than just words on a page.

18. Hearing poetry aloud is fun and exciting.

19. Try to find a poetry slam in your town!

Multiple Subjects and Verbs

Some sentences have more than one subject. Others have more than one verb. Many sentences have more than one subject *and* more than one verb. The subjects in the following sentences have been labelled with an "S" and the verbs with a "V."

   S   V   V
He swam and fished this summer.

       S   S   V
The dog and kitten became good friends.

   S   V   S   V
She danced well, and the director applauded.

       S V   S   V
When we study hard, we usually do well.

You can identify the pattern of a sentence by indicating how many subjects and verbs it has. In theory, a sentence can have any number of subjects and verbs, but these are the most common patterns:

S–V   one subject and one verb

S–V–V   one subject and two verbs

S–S–V   two subjects and one verb

S–V/S–V   two subjects and two verbs

▶ Underline the subjects of the following sentences *once* and the verbs *twice*.

The parrot squawked loudly.

His job started early and ended quite late.

Gardening and decorating were Natalia's joys.

The team won the game, but the captain was not happy.

Any group of words that *contains at least one subject and one verb* is called a **clause.** A single sentence may have one clause or more than one clause.

S–V	one clause	The boy ate his pizza slice.
S–V–V	one clause	Sonya danced and sang.
S–S–V	one clause	The judge and the attorneys conferred.
S–V/S–V	two clauses	The dog barked, / and we laughed.
S–V–V/S–V	two clauses	He hiked and fished / when the sun rose.

Later in this book we will study the different types of clauses to understand how they determine punctuation. For now, the important thing is to learn to find all the subjects and verbs in each sentence.

Something to keep in mind when looking for multiple subjects and verbs is that the *length* of the sentence won't necessarily tell you whether the sentence has one clause or several clauses. Look at these two sentences:

She sang, but I danced. (How many clauses?)

The anxious, nervous young bride tripped on the stairs. (How many clauses?)

The first sentence is short—only five words—but it has two S–V patterns and, therefore, two clauses (*she sang,* but *I danced*). The second sentence is more than twice as long as the first, but it has only one clause (*bride . . . tripped*). So don't be fooled by the length of the sentence: Some short sentences have multiple subjects and verbs, and some long sentences have only a single clause (S–V).

▶ The sentences below are skeleton sentences. That is, they are stripped down to only subjects, verbs, and connecting words. Go through them, underlining the subjects *once* and the verbs *twice*.

Joseé laughed and joked.

Julia and Ben argued and fought.

The poet, the artist, and the teacher spoke.

After the hockey game ended, we had lunch.

Laughter invigorates, and love binds.

Because it snowed, we stayed home.

When the movie ended, we left.

The philosopher and his ideas were exciting.

As we watched and waited, the river flooded.

If you go, I stay.

Tai wrote and revised.

As we listened, the storyteller entranced us.

He cried while she packed.

Watch your spelling! (Did you remember to put *You* in front?)

The practice sentences below have multiple subjects and verbs, but they also include the other types of words you studied in Chapter 1. Before you try them, review that chapter quickly to remind yourself about **adverbs** and **infinitives,** which are never part of the verb, and about **adjectives** and **possessives,** which
▶ are not part of the subject. Underline verbs *twice* and subjects *once*.

My uncles and aunts contribute to our family.

The long road seemed to run on for miles and miles.

Duane, José, and Georgio always loved to play soccer.

The gymnastic tournament finally ended, and the players went home.

After the spring semester ended, we partied a lot.

The terribly boring professor lectured monotonously to his class of students.

The boy's mother and father decided to send him to space camp.

The jury's verdict gladdened and relieved us.

The story's ending surprised us, but we still liked it.

Our new, fancy, expensive car has a CD player and a sun roof.

Keep off the grass, and don't pick the flowers!

EXERCISE 2A

▶ Underline the subjects of the following sentences *once* and the verbs *twice*. To help you, the pattern of each sentence is indicated in parentheses.

1. Few people know the story of Baron Alexander von Humboldt's life, but his name is very familiar to geographers. (S–V/S–V)

2. Eight townships in North America have the name Humboldt City, and California also named a county and a bay after him. (S–V/S–V)

3. Meteorologists in the Southern Hemisphere often mention his name in their weather forecasts because of the Humboldt Current. (S–V)

4. This cold water current flows along the west coast of South America and influences the weather there. (S–V–V)

5. Humboldt made important contributions to botany, geology, astronomy, and geography and also helped to create the fields of geomagnetism, climatology, oceanography, and ethnography. (S–V–V)

6. Some people describe him as "the last universal scholar in the field of natural sciences," and other writers call him "the most curious man in history." (S–V/S–V)

7. From 1799 to 1804, he went on expeditions through South America, Mexico, and the Caribbean. (S–V)

8. He observed and wrote about the cultures of the Incas and the Aztecs. (S–V–V)

9. His companion on the trip was Aime Bonpland, a French physician. (S–V)

10. Humboldt and Bonpland had exciting adventures in South America. (S–S–V)

11. They travelled down crocodile-infested rivers and climbed active volcanoes. (S–V–V)

12. Even if the situation was dangerous, they always carried their scientific instruments with them. (S–V/S–V)

13. They used these instruments when they climbed Chimborazo, an extremely steep mountain in Ecuador. (S–V/S–V)

14. Although Humboldt's hands were bloody from holding the mountain's sharp rocks, he still stopped to take scientific measurements. (S–V/S–V)

15. Humboldt's exploits attracted the attention of the American president Thomas Jefferson. (S–V)

16. Jefferson greatly admired Humboldt's accomplishments, and the two men enjoyed a lifelong friendship. (S–V/S–V)

17. At the end of his life, Humboldt reviewed his career and published the results of his scientific studies in a book. (S–V–V)

18. Because his scientific interests included so many different fields, Humboldt gave his book the very appropriate title of *Cosmos*. (S–V/S–V)

EXERCISE 2B

▶ Underline the subjects of the following sentences *once* and the verbs *twice*. Some sentences may have more than one subject, more than one verb, or both.

1. Around the world today, different countries finally agree on what time it is.

2. But few people know that it was a Canadian immigrant, Sandford Fleming, who created a universal standard time.

3. He became known as "The Father of Standard Time," and by 1929 countries worldwide accepted his system.

4. Fleming was born in Scotland and arrived in Canada at age seventeen.

5. He founded the Royal Canadian Institute in Toronto in 1819 to meet with other men who were scientists and thinkers.

6. He was a creative thinker, inventor, and scientist, and he even designed an early in-line skate around 1850.

7. Fleming's mind worked in many directions, for he designed the first Canadian postage stamp in 1851, a three-penny stamp featuring the beaver.

8. The beaver later became the national animal symbol for hard-working Canadians and for a land that was rich in lumber and water resources.

9. Sandford Fleming, among his many occupations, was a surveyor and mapmaker.

10. He proposed a railway running from sea to sea across Canada, which was then called British North America.

11. Almost fifteen years later, after Confederation, the government asked him to survey the route for a national railroad.

12. Fleming completed the survey in 1876, and the Canadian Pacific Railway began to become a reality.

13. In his role as surveyor, Fleming recommended safer iron bridges instead of wooden ones for the many bridges that spanned rivers and gorges.

14. He was present at the Canadian Pacific Railway's ceremony of "The Last Spike," which signalled the railway's completion in 1885.

15. By that time he was retired and was a board member for the railway company.

16. He had travelled across the country and explored many areas, which he mapped.

17. Queen's University in Kingston, Ontario, appointed Fleming Chancellor in 1880, and several campuses and a college in Ontario now bear his name.

18. A prodigious thinker and active man, even in his retirement he worked to get governments across the British Empire to construct underwater telegraph cables.

19. His dream came true, and in 1902 workers completed the "All Red Line" linking the British Empire.

20. Perhaps we remember him best as a man who brought people together across distances.

21. Although he was born in Scotland, Sandford Fleming, the Canadian, helped to unite a new nation.

22. He was a man of science, an engineer, and an inventor, and he made significant contributions to a growing country.

23. Sir Sandford was also a very community-minded person, and he deeded his home and his property in Halifax to the city.

24. The property became the large and beautiful Dingle Park, where citizens and tourists walk and enjoy the gardens.

25. Queen Victoria knighted this great Canadian Sir Sandford Fleming when she celebrated her Diamond Jubilee in 1897.

Prepositions

...etween
...sitions

a

One of the most common causes of errors in identifying the subject of a sentence is confusing it with a noun used as the object of a preposition. This kind of error can also lead to mistakes in subject–verb agreement. (Subject–verb agreement is covered in Unit 2 of this book.) To avoid making this type of mistake, you first must learn to recognize prepositions and prepositional phrases.

Prepositions are the short words in our language that show the *position* or relationship between one word and another. For example, if you were trying to describe where a particular store was located, you might say:

The store is *on* the right.

The store is *near* the highway.

The store is *by* the bank.

The store is *under* the elm tree.

The store is *behind* the garage.

The italicized words are all prepositions. They indicate the position of the store in relation to the right, the highway, the bank, the elm tree, and the garage.

Here is a list of the most common prepositions. You do not have to memorize these words, but you must be able to recognize them as prepositions when you see them.

about	between	of
above	beyond	on
across	by	onto
after	concerning	out
against	down	over
along	during	through
amid	except	to
among	for	toward
around	from	under
at	in	up
before	inside	upon
behind	into	with
below	like	within
beneath	near	without
beside		

As you can see from the example sentences describing the location of the store, prepositions are not used by themselves; they are always placed in front of a noun or a pronoun. The noun or pronoun following the preposition is called the **object of the preposition.** The group of words containing the preposition and its object is called a **prepositional phrase.** Any words, such as adjectives or the words *a, an,* or *the,* that come between the preposition and its object are also part of the prepositional phrase. Read the following sentences, in which the prepositional phrases are italicized. Notice that each prepositional phrase begins with a preposition and ends with a noun or a pronoun.

I leaned *against the car.*

He walked *toward the nearest exit.*

The glass *of orange juice* costs fifty cents.

She stood *beside me.*

Some prepositional phrases may have more than one object.

You may sit *near Sergei or Tran.*

You may have some *of the bread or waffles.*

It is also possible to have two or more prepositional phrases in a row.

We looked *for the clues in the forest.*

The director *of that movie at the local theatre* is sitting *by us.*

▶ Circle the prepositional phrases in the following sentences. Some sentences may have more than one prepositional phrase.

The policeman looked carefully around the room.

The keys to the car are in the glove compartment.

I gave your recipe to my next-door neighbour.

Ruth came to the party with me.

▶ Construct sentences of your own containing prepositional phrases. Use the prepositions listed below. Make certain that each of your sentences contains at least one subject and one verb.

with: _____

through: _____

by: _____

of: _____

at: _____

The words *before* and *after* may be used either as prepositions or as conjunctions (see below). If the word is being used as a preposition, it will be followed by a noun or pronoun object. If the word is being used as a conjunction, it will be followed by both a subject and a verb.

As a Preposition	*As a Conjunction*
I go to bed *before midnight*.	*Before* you leave the house, be sure to lock the door.
Ajay entered the room *after me*.	*After* the bell rang, the students left the room.

What do prepositional phrases have to do with identifying subjects and verbs? The answer is simple.

Any word that is part of a prepositional phrase cannot be the subject or the verb of a sentence.

This rule works for two reasons:

1. Any noun or pronoun in a prepositional phrase must be the object of the preposition, and the object of a preposition cannot also be a subject.
2. Prepositional phrases never contain verbs.

To see how this rule can help you identify subjects and verbs, read the following seventeen-word sentence:

At the height of the rush hour, my car stalled in the middle of a busy intersection.

If you want to find the subject and the verb of this sentence, you know that they will not be part of any of the sentence's prepositional phrases, so cross out all the prepositional phrases in the sentence.

~~At the height of the rush hour~~, my car stalled ~~in the middle of a busy intersection~~.

You now have only three words left out of the original seventeen, and you know that the subject and the verb must be within these three words. What are the subject and the verb?

▶ Read the following sentence, and cross out all of its prepositional phrases.

In the evening she works on her assignments for the next day.

If you crossed out all the prepositional phrases, you should be left with only two words—the subject *she* and the verb *works*.

▶   Identify the subject and the verb in the following sentence. Cross out the prepositional phrases first.

On the way to their hotel, a group of tourists stopped at a souvenir shop.

If you have identified all of the prepositional phrases, you should be left with only three words—*a group* and *stopped*. Which word is the subject, and which is the verb?

Now you can see another reason why it is important to be able to identify prepositional phrases. It might seem logical for the subject of the sentence to be *tourists*. However, because *of tourists* is a prepositional phrase, *tourists* cannot be the subject. Instead, the subject is *group*.

What is the subject of the following sentence?

Many members of Parliament are lawyers.

If you crossed out the prepositional phrase *of Parliament,* you would know that the subject is *members,* not *Parliament.*

▶   Underline the subjects of the following sentences *once* and the verbs *twice.* Remember to cross out the prepositional phrases first.

During the oil shortage, the price of gas increased.

The car with the dented fender belongs to Carolyn.

A house in the Beach in Toronto with three bedrooms and two bathrooms sells for more than $800,000.

The stores in the mall open at ten in the morning.

The driver of the red Corvette skidded into the centre lane.

One of the employees received a $50 raise.

Your clothes from the dry cleaner are in the closet.

EXERCISE 3A

▶ Underline the subjects of the following sentences *once* and the verbs *twice*. Some sentences may have more than one subject, more than one verb, or both. Remember to cross out the prepositional phrases first.

1. During a search of the Internet, I discovered a breed of dog with a very interesting history.

2. Its official name is the American Indian dog.

3. This dog still exists today, but the origin of the breed dates back twelve thousand years to the early Native American inhabitants of North and South America.

4. The ancestors of the American Indian dog came across the Bering Strait from Asia with their Native American masters.

5. In North America, Native American tribes bred this dog with the American coyote to produce a new breed.

6. Centuries of careful breeding produced highly intelligent and loyal animals.

7. For thousands of years, tribes used these dogs for hunting, for guarding, and even for pulling the family's belongings on a travois (an "A"-shaped frame).

8. However, after the introduction of the horse, these dogs became less important and were close to extinction only a few years ago.

9. The preservation of this breed is due largely to the efforts of Russell "Kim" LaFlamme.

10. LaFlamme used a core group of dogs from a Canadian tribe and from a village in the American Southwest to start a breeding program.

11. The purpose of the program was to increase the number of purebred American Indian dogs and to establish standards for their appearance.

12. Although these dogs resemble wolves or coyotes in appearance, they are much more gentle in nature.

13. The colour of their eyes ranges from blue to yellow to amber.

14. It is even possible for these dogs to have eyes of two different colours.

15. To recall the Native American heritage of these dogs, their owners sometimes give them fanciful names.

16. Names on record include Ghost Dancer, Star Gazer, and Little Sky.

17. Preserving breeds like the American Indian Dog gives us a link to the past.

18. It provides a way to remember the ancient inhabitants of North and South America, and their way of life.

19. If you want to learn more about this breed of dog, information is available on the Internet at the "American Indian Dog" website.

EXERCISE 3B

▶ Underline the subjects of the following sentences *once* and the verbs *twice*. Some sentences may have more than one subject, more than one verb, or both. Remember to cross out the prepositional phrases first.

1. One of the most popular attractions in select zoos around the world is the giant panda.

2. With their distinctive teddy-bear-like appearance, pandas always attract large crowds.

3. A mountainous region in southwestern China is the home of the giant panda.

4. Pandas live in dense bamboo forests at altitudes of between 1,500 and 3,000 metres.

5. The great majority of a panda's diet (99 percent) consists of bamboo.

6. To stay healthy, pandas need to eat nearly 18 kilograms of bamboo each day.

7. Eating this huge amount of bamboo occupies about fourteen hours of each panda's day.

8. This reliance on a single item of food creates a threat to the pandas' survival.

9. In the past, pandas travelled freely from one mountaintop to another in search of bamboo.

10. Now people inhabit most of the valleys between the mountains.

11. Because pandas are very shy, they avoid areas with people.

12. As people continue to farm and to cut timber at higher and higher elevations, the pandas' habitat shrinks.

13. With no route to new supplies of bamboo, many pandas starve to death.

14. At the present time, only one thousand pandas remain in China, and their extinction is a real possibility.

15. To help solve this problem, the Chinese built centres to breed pandas in captivity.

16. China also lends pairs of pandas to zoos around the world.

17. In Canada, the zoo in Toronto, Ontario, received pandas on loan in 1985.

18. If the pandas mate and produce offspring, the zoos get to keep the baby pandas for a year or two.

19. Eventually, however, the zoos return the parent pandas and their offspring to China.

20. This worldwide exchange of pandas helps to increase the number of animals and to educate the public about the threats to the pandas' existence.

21. After visits to panda exhibits in zoos, many people contribute money to wildlife organizations.

22. These organizations fund programs to save pandas and other animals in danger of extinction.

23. In this way, the popularity of pandas helps to preserve many other animals besides the pandas themselves.

Main Verbs and Helping Verbs

Verbs can be either **main verbs** or **helping** (also called **auxiliary**) **verbs.** Main verbs are the kind of verb you have already studied. Main verbs tell what action is being performed in a sentence. For example,

I *drive* to work each day.

This restaurant *serves* Portuguese food.

Helping verbs are used in combination with main verbs. They perform two major functions:

1. Helping verbs indicate shades of meaning that cannot be expressed by a main verb alone. Consider the differences in meaning in the following sentences, in which the helping verbs have been italicized.

I *may* marry you soon.   I *must* marry you soon.

I *should* marry you soon.   I *can* marry you soon.

As you can see, changing the helping verb changes the meaning of the entire sentence. These differences in meaning could not be expressed simply by using the main verb, *marry,* alone.

2. Helping verbs also show tense—the time at which the action of the verb takes place. Notice how changing the helping verb in the following sentences helps change the tense of the main verb *visit.* (Both the helping verbs and the main verbs have been italicized.)

He *is visiting* New York.

He *will visit* New York.

He *has visited* New York.

Notice the position that helping verbs have in a sentence. They always *come before* the main verb, although sometimes another word, such as an adverb, may come between the helping verb and the main verb.

The team *can win* the game.

The team *can* probably *win* the game.

You *should stay* in bed today.

You *should* definitely *stay* in bed today.

If a question contains a helping verb, the helping verb still *comes before* the main verb.

Can the team *win* the game?

Should you *stay* in bed today?

Does the car *run* well?

When *is* the plane *departing?*

The following words are special helping verbs often called modals. They help to express ability, condition, or necessity. Memorize them.

can, could

may, might, must

shall, should

will, would

The following words can be used either as helping verbs or as main verbs. They are helping verbs if they are used in combination with a main verb. They are main verbs if they occur alone. Memorize them.

has, have, had (forms of the verb *have*)

does, do, did, done (forms of the verb *do*)

am, is, are, was, were, been (forms of the verb *be*)

As Main Verbs	**As Helping Verbs**
He *has* my book.	He *has gone* home.
She *did* a headstand.	She *did* not *arrive* on time.
We *are* hungry.	We *are eating* soon.

From now on, whenever you are asked to identify the verbs in a sentence, *include all the main verbs and all the helping verbs*. For example, in the sentence "We should review this lesson," the complete verb is "should review." In the sentence "He has lost his wallet," the verb is "has lost." Underline the complete verbs in the following sentences.

Daniella must borrow some money.

I may go to Halifax this summer.

Sheila can speak German fluently.

We are leaving soon.

Some sentences may contain more than one helping verb.

one helping verb	The mechanic *is working* on your car.
two helping verbs	He *must have lost* your phone number.
three helping verbs	That bill *should have been paid* by now.

▶ Underline the subjects of the following sentences *once* and the complete verbs *twice*.

You could have sold your car for a better price.

The weather will be getting warmer soon.

You have not been listening to me.

Do you have a part-time job?

You should have gone to the dentist last week.

My cousin may be visiting me this summer.

Remember this rule:

The verbs in a sentence include all the main verbs plus all the helping verbs.

EXERCISE 4A

▶ Underline the subjects of the following sentences *once* and the verbs *twice*. Some sentences may have more than one subject, more than one set of verbs, or both. Remember to cross out prepositional phrases first.

1. Have you heard of the Jindo dog?

2. The Jindo is protected under Korean law because it has been designated as Korea's 53rd national monument.

3. This dog has had a very interesting history.

4. The Jindo is named after Jindo Island, off the coast of Korea.

5. Until recently, this island was separated from the Korean mainland by a powerful ocean current.

6. Because of the island's isolation, this breed was not officially recognized until the 20th century.

7. During the 1930s, Korea was occupied by Japan, and a Japanese professor became aware of this special dog.

8. The professor was impressed by the Jindo's intelligence and loyalty to its master.

9. However, intelligence in a dog can be a problem, for very intelligent dogs are also very independent.

10. Jindos will listen only to their masters, and sometimes they will not obey even their masters' commands.

11. They can outsmart most other dogs and will also try to outwit their owners.

12. Jindos are strongly attached to their homes, and people have found it difficult to relocate them.

13. For example, Jindos have been known to jump off ferryboats in order to swim back to their island home.

14. When owners in other parts of the world move, Jindos sometimes travel as far as 200 kilometres to return to their old homes.

15. Jindos were first brought to North America by American soldiers after the Korean War.

16. Although Jindos were meant to be pets, some disreputable people have bred the Jindo with vicious breeds.

17. These mixed breeds are then used in commercial dog fights.

18. The original Jindo, however, remains a good pet if its owner can tolerate its independent ways.

EXERCISE 4B

▶ Underline the subjects of the following sentences *once* and the verbs *twice*. Some sentences may have more than one subject, more than one set of verbs, or both. Remember to cross out prepositional phrases first.

1. The North American diet has traditionally included far more meat than fish.

2. However, eating fish is becoming increasingly popular.

3. Fish have fewer calories than some kinds of meat, and they also contain important nutrients.

4. In order to increase the supply of seafood, fish are now being raised on commercial fish farms.

5. However, commercial fish farming can create problems as well as benefits.

6. Salmon are a very popular fish, and they are raised in farms along the ocean coasts.

7. However, growing a large number of fish in a small area allows parasites and diseases to flourish.

8. Antibiotics must then be given to the salmon to keep them free of disease.

9. Overuse of these antibiotics has created drug-resistant strains of disease.

10. These new diseases may eventually infect fish both on farms and in the wild.

11. Pesticides are applied to keep the fish pens free of algae.

12. Poisonous chemicals from these pesticides are now accumulating on the ocean floor and are polluting the water.

13. In the wild, salmon can feed on a variety of plants and small organisms.

14. On commercial farms, they are fed artificial food in the form of protein pellets.

15. Chemicals in this food can cause cancer if people eat the fish in large amounts.

16. For this reason, the Canadian government has advised the public not to eat salmon from fish farms more than once a month.

17. An additional problem is created when waste products from the fish decay on the ocean bottom.

18. The process of decay consumes large quantities of oxygen, and a shortage of oxygen could lead to the death of nearby shellfish and other bottom-dwellers.

19. The salmon in fish farms do not come from the same species as salmon in the wild.

20. If farm salmon escape, they may compete with wild salmon for food and territory.

21. The presence of a different species will upset the balance of nature and could lead to a reduction in the number of wild salmon.

22. Commercial fish farms do make fish more available to the public at a lower price.

23. However, they can also present dangers to people's health and to the environment.

Unit 1 Review

▶ Underline the subjects of the following sentences *once* and the complete verbs *twice*. Some sentences may have more than one subject, more than one verb, or both.

1. Cattle have played an important role in human life for thousands of years.

2. Pictures of ancient cattle appear in cave paintings from thirty thousand years ago.

3. The ancestors of modern cattle were called aurochs.

4. They were larger than today's cattle, and one of these animals could feed an entire band of people.

5. Their meat was roasted over an open fire, and this custom survives in today's barbecue.

6. Cattle were domesticated about eight thousand years ago when humans began to live in one place and grow crops.

7. Humans do not have the ability to digest grass, but cattle can convert grass into meat and milk for human consumption.

8. In addition to meat and milk, cattle are a source of power to pull plows, and their hides can be made into leather.

9. Their manure makes a good fertilizer for crops, and in areas with few trees, people may also use the manure as fuel.

10. The importance of cattle can be seen in the lives of two different societies.

11. The lives of the Masai tribe in Kenya are centred on the raising of cattle.

12. A Masai man must buy his bride from his wife's family, and the price is thirty or more cattle.

13. Milk is a staple of the Masai diet and is often drunk with each meal.

14. Because milk is so important, cattle are butchered only on special occasions.

15. The best cuts of meat are reserved for the elder members of the group and for the warriors.

16. The women and children are served last.

17. Among the Masai, the gift of a cow in a time of need is considered an act of true charity.

18. One group of Masai offered to send cattle to New York after they heard about the September 11, 2001, attacks on the city.

19. In India, cattle are regarded as holy, and they are brought to a new building to bless it.

20. Many Indian cattle live and work on farms, but some cattle also roam freely on the streets of nearby towns.

21. These urban animals have adapted their diets to survive on garbage, such as rotting fruits and vegetables.

22. Their remarkable stomachs can digest even newspapers and cardboard boxes.

23. India has an annual holiday to honour cattle and to thank them for all their contributions to human life.

24. The cattle are bathed, and they are decorated with paint and floral garlands.

25. On this one day, they are allowed to wander through the marketplaces and to eat freely from the piles of food for sale.

26. It is difficult to imagine a world without cattle and without the products from these useful animals.

Unit

2

Subject–Verb Agreement

Recognizing Singular and Plural Subjects and Verbs

Errors in **subject–verb** agreement are among the most common grammatical mistakes. By applying the rules in this unit, you should be able to correct many of the errors in your own writing. As you already know, a sentence must contain both a subject and a verb. Read the following two sentences. What is the grammatical difference between them?

The bank opens at ten o'clock in the morning.

The banks open at ten o'clock in the morning.

In the first sentence, the subject *bank* is singular. **Singular** means "one." There is one bank in the first sentence. In the second sentence, the subject *banks* is plural. **Plural** means "two or more." There are at least two (and possibly more than two) banks in the second sentence.

Like the subject *bank*, the verb *opens* in the first sentence is singular. Verb forms ending in -*s* are used with *singular* subjects, as in the sentence "The bank *opens* at ten o'clock in the morning." The verb *open* in the second sentence above is plural. This verb form (without a final -*s*) is used with *plural* subjects, as in the sentence "The banks *open* at ten o'clock in the morning."

In other words, if the subject of a sentence is *singular,* the verb in the sentence must also be *singular.* If the subject of the sentence is *plural,* the verb must be in its *plural* form. This matching of singular subjects with singular verbs and plural subjects with plural verbs is called **subject–verb agreement.**

To avoid making mistakes in subject–verb agreement, you must be able to recognize the difference between singular and plural subjects and verbs.

The subjects of sentences are usually nouns or pronouns. As you know, the plurals of nouns are usually formed by adding an -*s* to singular forms.

Singular	*Plural*
envelope	envelopes
restaurant	restaurants

However, a few nouns (under 1 percent) have irregular plural forms.

Singular	*Plural*
man	men
leaf	leaves
child	children
thesis	theses
self	selves
medium	media (as in the "mass media")

Pronouns that can be used as subjects are also singular or plural, depending on whether they refer to one or more than one person, place, or thing.

Singular	*Plural*
I	we
you	you
he, she, it	they

Notice that the pronoun *you* may be either singular or plural.

If nouns show number by adding -*s* to the plural, what do verbs do to show whether a verb is singular or plural? A long time ago, English verbs had many different endings for this purpose, but most of those endings have been dropped. Today most English verbs look the same whether the subject is singular or plural: "I talk," "we talk," "the men talk," "I remembered," "they remembered," "the class remembered," and so on. However, there is one place where English verbs have kept a special ending to show number. That special ending is also an -*s,* and the place where it is added is in the present-tense singular with the subject pronouns *he, she, it* and with any singular noun that could replace any of these pronouns. Look at these sentences written in the present tense, and notice when the -*s* is added to the verb:

Singular	*Plural*
I talk.	We talk.
You talk.	You talk.
He talks.	They talk.
She talks.	They talk.
It talks.	They talk.
The man talks.	The men talk.
The girl talks.	The girls talk.

To sum up, although adding an -*s* to most nouns (99 percent) makes them plural, some singular verbs also end with an -*s.* Verbs in the present tense, third-person singular (*he, she, it*) always end in -*s.* An easy way to remember this difference is to memorize this rule:

Any verb ending in -*s* is singular.

There are no exceptions to this rule. Therefore, it is not good usage in academic writing to have a sentence in which a plural subject is matched with a verb ending in -*s.*

Effective writers are as aware of **usage** as they are of grammar. Good usage means choosing different kinds of language for different situations, just as we choose different clothes for different occasions. In **informal** situations, such as conversations with friends, it is common to choose informal usage. However, almost all of the writing you do for college is in **formal** situations, such as exams and essay assignments. The difference between formal and informal usage can be seen when we make subjects agree with their verbs. Because most conversation is very informal, you may have heard or have used many informal verb choices in your own conversations. Notice the differences in usage in these examples:

Informal	*Formal*
We was here.	We were here.
He don't come here.	He doesn't come here.
They was at the beach.	They were at the beach.

You want your academic writing to be as effective as you can make it. In college you must choose **formal usage** in almost every situation—essays, reports, exams, and so on. The exercises in this book are *always* designed for you to choose formal usage.

To avoid subject–verb agreement errors, there are some rules that you should keep in mind. (How you "keep rules in mind" is up to you. If you find that even after you study rules, you still cannot remember them, you should *memorize* the rules in this unit.)

Rule 1. A verb agrees with the subject, not with the complement. A **complement** is a word that refers to the same person or thing as the subject of the sentence. It follows a linking verb.

                    S   LV   C
Our main economic *problem is* rising prices.

In the sentence above, the subject is *problem,* which is singular. The subject is not *prices.* Rather, *prices* is the complement. Therefore, the linking verb takes the singular form *is* to agree with *problem.* If the sentence is reversed, it reads:

                    S   LV   C
Rising *prices are* our main economic problem.

The subject is now the plural noun *prices,* and *problem* is the complement. The verb now takes the plural form *are.* Which are the correct verbs in the following sentences?

The topic of discussion (was, were) political refugees.

Astrological signs (seems, seem) to be an interesting subject to many people.

Rule 2. Prepositional phrases have no effect on a verb.

The *president* of the company, with his chief economic advisers, is having a press conference today.

In the sentence above, the subject is singular (*president*). The prepositional phrases, *of the company,* and *with his chief economic advisers,* have no effect on the verb, which remains singular (*is having*).

A hamburger with French fries costs five dollars.

The singular verb *costs* agrees with the singular subject *hamburger.* The prepositional phrase *with French fries* has no effect on the verb. Which is the correct verb in the following sentence?

The woman with her ten cats (was, were) evicted for breaking the clause in her lease that prohibited the keeping of pets.

In addition, do not mistakenly make your verb agree with a noun or pronoun in a prepositional phrase. (This is easy to do because many prepositional phrases come just before a verb.)

The *problems* of this school district *trouble* the school board greatly.

In the sentence above, the subject is plural (*problems*). The plural verb *trouble* agrees with *problems*, not with the singular object of the preposition (*district*).

The attitude of adolescents is often difficult to understand.

The singular verb *is* agrees with the singular subject *attitude*, not with the plural object of the preposition (*adolescents*).

▶ Which are the correct verbs in the following sentences? Remember to cross out the prepositional phrases to identify the subject and verb more clearly.

One of the restaurants (serves, serve) Thai food.

The directions for the test (was, were) confusing.

Among the many guests, he (was, were) the tallest.

Rule 3. Be especially alert for subject–verb agreement when the sentence has **inverted word order,** as in these three situations:

a) **Questions**

Notice the location of the subject in these questions:

HV S MV
Does he want a new car? (subject between helping and main verb)

V S
Is turkey your favourite food? (subject after main verb)

Interrogative words like *when, where,* and *how* come at the beginning of sentence patterns, but they are never subjects.

    HV   S   MV
When *does* the *game start?* (subject between helping and main verb)

     MV   S
Where *is* the *picnic?* (subject after verb)

       HV S MV

How *can he study* all weekend? (subject between helping and main verb)

b)   Sentence patterns beginning with *here* or *there*

The words *here* and *there* are never subjects. They are called *fillers*.
Notice the location of the subject in these patterns:

There *are* many *children* here today. (subject after verb)

Here *are* your test *results*. (subject after verb)

You may check that you are correct by changing the word order:

Many *children are* here today.

Your test *results are* here.

c)   Rare patterns in which the verb precedes the subject

Occasionally a writer will, for emphasis, put a subject after its verb.
Notice the location of the subject in these sentences:

Behind the lamp in the corner *was* the very expensive *statue*. (If the order of
this sentence were reversed, it would read, "The very expensive statue was
behind the lamp in the corner.")

Toward the finish line *raced* the breathless *runner*. ("The breathless runner
raced toward the finish line.")

EXERCISE 5A

▶ Circle the verb that correctly completes each sentence. Make certain that you cross out prepositional phrases and that you have identified the correct subject.

1. Visiting art museums (is, are) a favourite pastime for many people.

2. The focus of most museum collections (is, are) traditional art forms, such as painting and sculpture.

3. However, on the edge of the art world, new types of art (exists, exist).

4. Computer games, with their extraordinary graphics, (is, are) one of these new art forms.

5. These games (was, were) the subject of a popular exhibit at the Los Angeles County Museum of Art.

6. Finding exhibits of computer graphics in an art exhibit (comes, come) as a surprise to more traditional museum visitors.

7. However, to some scholars and critics, the beauty of computer games (equals, equal) that of more traditional visual objects.

8. There (is, are) even universities that offer courses in computer games as part of their curriculum.

9. One of these schools (is, are) the University of Alberta; it even has a post-doctoral research group in the use of artificial intelligence in video games.

10. In these new courses, the literary aspect of computer games, as well as their computer science and design graphics, (is, are) studied.

11. The literary approach to computer games (focuses, focus) on their narrative structure.

12. The narrative design of these games (opens, open) up new possibilities for story development.

13. Built into the structure of a computer game story (is, are) a choice of several different plot outcomes.

14. Thus, the person playing the game, along with the game's designer, (determines, determine) how the story evolves.

15. Of course, to some computer game developers, the primary purpose of computer games (is, are) to provide entertainment, rather than literature or art.

16. (Does, Do) these kinds of academic discussions (interests, interest) the typical game player?

17. Perhaps all their hours in front of a computer screen (serves, serve) as a preparation for eventual college degrees!

18. It is interesting to know that there (is, are) more than one way to look at a subject.

19. Viewing things from multiple perspectives (broadens, broaden) our horizons and helps to make us comfortable with the changing times.

EXERCISE 5B

▶ Some of the sentences in this exercise contain subject–verb agreement errors. Others are correct as written. If a sentence contains an agreement error, cross out the incorrect verb, and write the correct verb in its place. If the sentence has no agreement errors, mark it C for *correct*.

1. Among the world's most beautiful natural objects are the pearl.

2. The pearl's beauty, along with its scarcity, have made people value it as a jewel for thousands of years.

3. In ancient Rome, a strand of pearls were the ultimate status symbol for wealthy women.

4. Of course, the availability of cultured pearls make it possible for pearl jewellery to be sold at reasonable prices now.

5. The formation of natural pearls are caused by an irritant, such as a grain of sand, lodging in an oyster's soft tissues.

6. Pearls are the result of the oyster's attempt to protect its tissues from further damage.

7. The oyster secretes a substance called nacre and use the nacre to form a protective coating around the foreign object.

8. The accumulation of layers of nacre eventually form what we call a pearl.

9. In the production of cultured pearls, beads made from abalone shells is used as the irritant.

10. The placement of these beads in the oysters are called "seeding"; each oyster must be individually seeded by hand.

11. The growing period for cultured pearls last from one to four years.

12. The value of the pearls increase the longer the pearl is allowed to grow.

13. There are a combination of factors that affect a pearl's price.

14. One of the most important of these factors is a pearl's lustre or sheen.

15. The thickness of a pearl's layers are a major factor in determining its sheen.

16. More layers of nacre also increases the pearl's size, with larger pearls usually costing more.

17. The price of pearls also depend on their shape.

18. Only one in a hundred pearls are perfectly round, so their scarcity makes them valuable.

19. There are a range of colour choices available for pearls.

20. Selecting a colour depends on the complexion of the person wearing the pearls.

21. For example, a pearl with pink tones look best on fair complexions while an ivory-coloured pearl flatters darker complexions.

22. Finally, the surface of pearls influence their price.

23. Among the possible imperfections in a pearl's surface are dark or rough spots.

24. Do jewellery made of pearls appeal to you?

Indefinite Pronouns as Subjects

The subject pronouns we have been studying, like *she* or *it* or *they*, refer to specific, definite persons, places, or things. This chapter is about another kind of pronoun, **indefinite pronouns**, which do not refer to a specific person or place or to definite things.

Rule 4. The following indefinite pronouns are **singular** and require **singular** verbs:

anybody, anyone, anything

each, each one

either, neither

everybody, everyone, everything

nobody, no one, nothing

somebody, someone, something

Everybody has his camping gear.

Anything goes.

Each of the players *knows* the ground rules.

Either of those times *is* all right with me.

Notice that in the last two sentences, the verbs agree with the singular subjects *each* and *either*. The verbs are not affected by the plural nouns in the prepositional phrases *of the players* or *of those times*.

Rule 5. Indefinite pronouns, such as the words *some, half, most,* and *all,* may take either singular or plural verbs, depending on their meaning in the context of the sentence. If these words tell **how much** of something is meant, the verb is singular; but if they tell **how many** of something is meant, the verb is plural.

Most of the bread *is* stale. (how much?)

Most of the actors *are* present. (how many?)

Some of the money *is* missing. (how much?)

Some of the players *were* late. (how many?)

All of the fortune *goes* to the family. (how much?)

All of these items *go* to us. (how many?)

Do not confuse the words in this rule with the words *each, either,* and *neither* in Rule 4. Those three words *always* require a singular verb.

Do not confuse the modifiers *much* and *many* with indefinite pronouns.

Many players choose to switch teams. (*Players* is the plural subject, which takes the plural verb *choose*.)

There was much confusion over the new rules. (*Confusion* is the singular subject, which takes the singular verb *was*.)

One of is a special expression. It requires a plural noun, but the verb agrees with the singular *one*.

One of (*singular*) the players (*plural noun*) was given (*singular verb*) a penalty for high sticking.

The teacher asks which one of (*singular*) the students (*plural noun*) is (*singular verb*) guilty.

EXERCISE 6A

▶ **Part 1:** Circle the verb that correctly completes each sentence. This exercise covers only rules from Chapter 6.

1. (Do, Does) everyone know the assignment for tomorrow?

2. Neither of those restaurants (is, are) accessible to people in wheelchairs.

3. Some of my classes (requires, require) buying extra materials in addition to textbooks.

4. Most of her salary (goes, go) toward paying for her rent, her food, and her car.

5. All of the desserts (needs, need) to be refrigerated immediately.

6. Each of the restaurants (offers, offer) a different kind of cuisine.

7. All of the furniture (is, are) on sale this week.

8. (Has, have) anyone forgotten to sign up for the trip?

▶ **Part 2:** Circle the verb that correctly completes each sentence. This exercise covers rules from Chapters 5 and 6.

9. Each of my friends (has, have) a favourite summer vacation spot.

10. Most of them (prefers, prefer) places with beautiful scenery and outdoor activities.

11. Generally, nobody (thinks, think) of a ski resort as a summer getaway.

12. However, one of the best choices for a summer vacation (is, are) a ski resort in British Columbia.

13. A combination of natural beauty, varied activities, and interesting shops (makes, make) the town of Whistler, B.C., a wonderful summer destination.

14. One of Whistler's major attractions (is, are) the beautiful Blackcomb Glacier.

15. The availability of outdoor sports, such as golf, hiking, fishing, and horseback riding, (adds, add) to the resort's appeal.

16. The high cost of lodgings (is, are) a problem at many popular resorts.

17. However, during the summer months, the availability of campgrounds (make, makes) accommodation much more affordable.

18. A family with children often (saves, save) money by camping or renting a condominium with a kitchen instead of eating every meal in a restaurant.

19. There (is, are) a wide selection of art galleries in the town.

20. Most of the art work (reflects, reflect) a mountain theme, with its seasonal changes.

21. Some of the galleries also (features, feature) work by First Nations and Inuit artists.

22. Everyone also (enjoys, enjoy) the live music in the plaza some afternoons and evenings.

23. All of these features (convinces, convince) our family to make a return visit.

24. Most of our holiday savings now (goes, go) into a special summer ski fund.

EXERCISE 6B

▶ Some of the sentences in this exercise contain subject–verb agreement errors. Others are correct as written. If a sentence contains an agreement error, cross out the incorrect verb, and write the correct one in its place. If a sentence has no agreement errors, mark it C for *correct*. This exercise covers rules from Chapters 5 and 6.

1. One of our nation's most popular tourist destinations are the Atlantic Provinces.

2. Is there anyone who haven't dreamed of dining on fresh lobster or fish in an ocean-view restaurant?

3. Four provinces makes up this beautiful region.

4. Each of these provinces have historical sites and beautiful National and Provincial parks.

5. The largest of these provinces are Newfoundland and Labrador, which is one province, but the linking of both names are sometimes confusing to newcomers.

6. The province of Newfoundland and Labrador have the site of an early Viking settlement at L'Anse aux Meadows.

7. Everybody who visit the site are amazed that the Norse farmed "Vinland," as they called it, 500 years before Columbus discovered the Americas.

8. L'Anse aux Meadows is one of UNESCO's World Heritage Sites, and are protected by Parks Canada.

9. Another popular tourist destination in the Atlantic Provinces are Cape Breton's Cabot Trail in the northern part of Nova Scotia.

10. Winding along the coast, this scenic drive take tourists along rocky cliffs, through fishing villages, down to sandy beaches and rocky coves where they can goes whale watching.

11. The trail, with all its natural attractions, are named after Giovanni Caboto, who is known as John Cabot because the English king sponsored his explorations in the 15th century.

12. Also in Cape Breton, the Alexander Graham Bell National Historic Park and the reconstructed Fortress of Louisbourg is favourite tourist attractions.

13. Farther west, the rugged coast of New Brunswick, with its picturesque inlets and bays, bring sightseers and artists.

14. New Brunswick's Kouchibouguac National Park boasts sand dunes, salt marshes, and tidal pools that draws many rare birds and the hikers and birdwatchers who come from afar to see them.

15. The name Kouchibouguac (*Koo-she-boo-joo-ak*) is Mi'kmaq and means "river of the long tides."

16. The tides creates many interesting phenomena throughout the Atlantic Provinces, and the tides of New Brunswick's Bay of Fundy has the highest tidal fluctuations in the world!

17. The smallest of these provinces are Prince Edward Island, famous for its potatoes, red beaches, and "Anne of Green Gables" shows at the annual Charlottetown Festival.

18. Some visitors take the ferry across the Northumberland Strait, but most now prefer to save time and drive across Confederation Bridge.

19. This bridge with two lanes, built in 1997, take visitors 13 kilometres across often ice-covered water, from the mainland to the island.

20. Going from one province to another throughout a trip allow visitors to get glimpses of the wonderful variety of natural attractions in the region.

21. The Atlantic Provinces' combination of natural beauty, cultural and historic heritage, and welcoming hosts make tourism one of the region's leading industries.

Subjects Understood in a Special Sense

This chapter discusses several small groups of words used as subjects that call for special attention in subject–verb agreement.

Rule 6. Some subjects, though **plural in form,** are **singular in meaning** and, therefore, require a singular verb. Such words include *news, mathematics, physics, economics, aeronautics, electronics, molasses, mumps,* and *measles.*

Economics was my least favourite class.

Mumps is a common disease among children.

Rule 7. A **unit of time, weight, measurement,** or **money** usually requires a singular verb because the entire amount is thought of as a single unit.

Twenty *dollars is* all the money I have.

Two *kilograms* of meat *feeds* six people.

Eighteen *metres* of cloth *completes* our fabric needs.

Three *weeks was* all they had for their vacation.

Rule 8. Collective nouns usually require singular verbs. A collective noun is a word that is singular in form but that refers to a group of people or things. Some common collective nouns are such words as *group, team, family, class, crowd,* and *committee.*

The *crowd is* very noisy.

The *committee holds* frequent meetings.

Occasionally, a collective noun may be used with a plural verb if the writer wishes to show that the members of the group are acting as separate individuals rather than as a unified body. Notice the difference in meaning between the following pair of sentences:

The *board of directors supports* the measure. (In this sentence, the *board of directors* is acting as a single, unified group.)

The *board of directors are divided* over whether to pass the measure. (In this sentence, the *board of directors* is viewed as a collection of separate individuals who, because they are not in agreement, are not acting as a unified group.)

EXERCISE 7A

▶ Circle the verb that correctly completes each sentence. This section of the exercise covers only the rules in Chapter 7.

1. Seventy-five dollars (is, are) a lot to pay for one textbook.

2. The museum's board of directors (meet, meets) once a month.

3. Two tablespoons of cooking oil (goes, go) into the cake recipe.

4. The evening news (continues, continue) to be filled with sad events.

5. Economics (is, are) a required course for business majors.

6. The university's board of trustees (is, are) divided on whether to raise student fees.

▶ The following sentences cover rules from Chapters 5–7.

7. The new board of our condominium association (plans, plan) to repave our parking lot.

8. The team usually (agrees, agree) about where to go for dinner after practice.

9. Most of the pop (is, are) in the cooler.

10. German measles (causes, cause) some birth defects.

11. A wagon of apples and various fruits (stands, stand) by the farmhouse.

12. Two hours (is, are) too long to wait for a doctor's appointment!

13. Two dollars a page (was, were) the charge for proofreading my essay.

14. (Is, Are) the class going to the opera as part of the assignment?

15. Neither of those movies (looks, look) good to me.

16. Some of the material for the dress (is, are) on sale at the fabric store.

17. (Has, Have) some of the jury members been able to reach a verdict?

18. Here (is, are) the list of open classes.

19. Neither of the classes (meets, meet) at a convenient time for me.

20. Economics (affects, affect) many areas of our lives.

21. The focus of today's lecture (is, are) the events leading to the Riel Rebellion.

22. Most of the information in the reporter's articles (comes, come) from an unnamed source.

23. (Has, Have) either of the stolen cars been recovered?

24. My cousin, along with her husband and children, (visits, visit) me each summer.

EXERCISE 7B

▶ Some of the sentences in this exercise contain subject–verb agreement errors. Others are correct as written. If a sentence contains an agreement error, cross out the incorrect verb, and write the correct form in its place. If a sentence has no agreement errors, mark it C for *correct*. This exercise covers the rules in Chapters 5–7.

1. Pierre Sauvé, along with his wife and two children, need to move to Vancouver because Pierre's company has transferred him there.

2. Among the most important tasks facing the Sauvé family are buying a new home.

3. The biggest problem with buying a home on the coast are the high prices.

4. A combination of too few homes for sale and low interest rates for mortgages have created a real estate boom.

5. In some areas of the city, the price of homes have increased by more than 10 percent in just one year.

6. Pierre was shocked to learn that 500 thousand dollars are the median price for a home in West Vancouver.

7. The Sauvés have only 300 thousand dollars to spend on a house, so most of the area's homes costs more than they can afford to pay.

8. There are a small choice of houses available in the Sauvés' price range, but all of these homes lack features that the family wants.

9. A home with at least three bedrooms are necessary for a family with both a son and a daughter, but each of the less expensive homes come with only two bedrooms.

10. Another one of the family's problems are finding a home in a school district offering French programs.

11. The Sauvés found two very old three-bedroom houses in their price range, but neither of the homes were located near such schools.

12. In addition, the new school semester starts in four weeks, and four weeks do not give the family much time to find a place to live.

13. Finally, the Sauvés' real estate agent said, "Here are some alternatives you should consider."

14. One of the realtor's suggestions are renting an apartment for a year to give the family more time to look for a house.

15. However, because the price of homes have been rising steadily, Pierre doesn't want to delay buying a house.

16. The realtor also says there are a supply of less expensive homes in outlying suburbs of the city.

17. Some of the housing in Surrey, for example, are within Pierre's price range.

18. Pierre learned he could commute on the light rapid transit system, saving time on the drive from the Lower Mainland, and avoids waiting at the bridge.

19. Unfortunately, economics determine many of the decisions in a family's life.

20. A choice between a convenient location and an affordable price face the Sauvé family.

21. An hour and a quarter a day are not too long for Pierre to spend commuting, so the Sauvés finally decide to buy a house in Surrey instead of one closer to the city centre.

22. The children, meanwhile, has become more involved in outdoor activities like cycling and hiking in their new surroundings.

Subjects Joined by Conjunctions

Subjects joined by conjunctions require the special rules in this chapter.

Rule 9. Two subjects joined by the conjunction *and* are plural and require a plural verb.

> *French* and *Italian are* both Romance languages.
>
> *Concordia University* and *York University* both *have* excellent film schools.

Rule 10. When *each, every,* or *any* is used as an adjective in front of subjects, the subjects that are modified require a singular verb. (Writers have the most trouble with this rule when the sentence has two or more subjects joined by *and,* so this rule is an exception to Rule 9, above.)

> *Each* boy and girl under the age of five *rides* the bus free of charge.
>
> *Every* Tom, Dick, and Harry *wants* to borrow money from me.

Notice that the adjectives *every* and *each* make the verbs in the sentences singular even though each sentence has more than one subject.

Rule 11. Two singular subjects joined by the conjunctions *or* or *nor* are singular and require a singular verb.

> Neither *Sharon* nor *Charlotte knows* the telephone number.
>
> *Monday* or *Tuesday is* my parents' anniversary.

Rule 12. If both a singular and a plural subject are joined by *or* or *nor,* the subject that is closer to the verb determines whether the verb is singular or plural.

> Either two *onions* or a *clove* of garlic *is* necessary for this recipe.
>
> Either a *clove* of garlic or two *onions are* necessary for this recipe.
>
> *Is* a *clove* of garlic or two *onions* necessary for this recipe?
>
> *Are* two *onions* or a *clove* of garlic necessary for this recipe?

(Note: In the final two sentences, it is the *helping* verb that agrees with the subject.)

EXERCISE 8A

▶ Circle the verb that correctly completes each sentence. This section of the exercise covers only the rules in Chapter 8.

1. Every man and woman in this company (competes, compete) on an equal footing.

2. Either the coach or her assistant (decides, decide) where the games should be played.

3. Each car and motorcycle (needs, need) to have current licence plates.

4. Recent box office hits show that good acting and a good storyline (contributes, contribute) more to a film's success than special effects.

5. Neither the teacher nor the students (was, were) consulted about the test results.

6. Neither the gymnasts nor their coach (has, have) been invited to the competition's closing ceremonies.

7. (Is, Are) a lemon or two limes required for the recipe?

8. Every stray dog and cat in the neighbourhood (seems, seem) to end up in my yard.

▶ Sentences 9–20 cover the rules in Chapters 5–8.

9. Two weeks of winter vacation (is, are) not enough time to truly relax.

10. (Do, Does) either of the dancers perform regularly?

11. Most of the meat (was, were) imported from Argentina.

12. (Is, Are) physics a required course for engineering school?

13. Beyond the meadow and near the river (is, are) some lovely campgrounds.

14. All of the ingredients for our dinner (is, are) on that table.

15. Either garlic toast or cornbread (comes, come) with your meal.

16. Two boxes of paper (was, were) delivered to our school.

17. Neither the flu nor a bad cold (keeps, keep) me from my exercise regimen.

18. The rock star and her entourage (sits, sit) in the front rows of the theatre.

19. Either a doctor or a nurse practitioner (needs, need) to sign this prescription.

20. Half of my medications (costs, cost) more than fifty dollars each.

21. Most of this store's merchandise (comes, come) from local factories.

22. A combination of high temperatures and high humidity (makes, make) the summer weather in my hometown unpleasant.

23. Each of the committees (has, have) different tasks to complete.

24. Just thirty minutes of brisk walking each day (improves, improve) the health of previously sedentary people.

EXERCISE 8B

▶ Some of the sentences in this exercise contain subject–verb agreement errors. Others are correct as written. If a sentence contains a subject–verb agreement error, cross out the incorrect verb, and write the *correct* form in its place. If a sentence has no agreement errors, label it C for *correct*. This exercise covers rules from Chapters 5–8.

1. There are a total of twelve animals in the Chinese zodiac system.

2. Each of these animals rule over one lunar year.

3. For example, 1900 and all other multiples of 12 after 1900 (1972, 1984, 1996, etc.) are years of the rat.

4. According to Chinese astrological theory, every man and woman born in a particular lunar year have the personality traits of that year's animal.

5. A combination of good and bad traits appear in all years.

6. For instance, honesty and ambition forms an important part of a rat person's character.

7. On the other hand, constant gossiping or sudden outbursts of anger also appears in the rat personality.

8. Among the reasons for consulting the Chinese zodiac are choosing the correct marriage partner.

9. Either a dragon person (1976, 1988, 2000) or a monkey person (1968, 1980, 1992) make a suitable mate for a rat person.

10. In contrast, the marriage of rat people and horse people (1978, 1990, 2002) almost guarantees disaster.

11. The most fortunate position in the Chinese calendar are occupied by dragon people, for the dragon is the most powerful of the twelve animals.

12. Some of the traits of a dragon person includes wealth, long life, and continual good luck.

13. The influence of the Chinese zodiac extends to other important areas of a person's life.

14. Even economics are affected because people may compare horoscopes before accepting new jobs or entering into business deals with potential partners.

15. One problem for English speakers are variations among the English-language descriptions of the Chinese zodiac.

16. Different books or websites offer slightly different lists of characteristics for each animal.

17. Of course, even some of the Chinese population no longer believe in traditional astrology.

18. Nevertheless, in Chinese communities all over the world, each and every lunar new year are celebrated as the year of a particular animal.

19. The year 2008 will be another Year of the Rat, so everyone with rat-year birthdays are wished an especially good year!

▶ Correct any subject–verb agreement errors that you find in the following paragraphs by crossing out the incorrect verbs and writing in the correct forms. It may help you to underline all the subjects in the sentences once and the verbs twice before you try to identify errors in agreement.

Among the problems facing busy people today are finding a convenient way to exercise regularly. In addition, a combination of athletic ability and physical strength are required to master most sports. However, one of the Asian martial arts are easy to learn, even for people who do not consider themselves athletic or who are not already in good physical shape. This martial art is tai chi chuan, commonly called tai chi (pronounced *tie-chee*).

Tai chi, unlike most other martial arts, emphasize slow, graceful movements. Sports-related injuries is a problem with many forms of exercise, but a sprained joint or sore muscles rarely occurs with tai chi. A single tai chi workout consist of up to 108 separate positions or forms. Each of these forms appear in a specific sequence, like the movements in a ballet. Every one of the movements are done only once, and fifteen minutes are enough time to complete the basic routine although some of the advanced routines requires more time.

Among the advantages of tai chi is its convenience and lack of expense. Neither special clothing nor equipment are necessary. An outfit of comfortable clothes and flat shoes are the only requirement. It also isn't necessary to travel to a special place to practise tai chi. An empty space with enough room to take four steps in each direction are all that is needed. Therefore, tai chi encourages exercising on a daily basis. Since neither a teammate nor a special practice area are needed, people can perform their tai chi routine whenever they have a few minutes of free time.

In China, where the sport originated, a common sight are people practising tai chi each morning in city parks. Some of these people is elderly, for a combination of health benefits make tai chi especially good for older adults. Tai chi can lower high blood pressure and reduce pain and stiffness in arthritic joints. In addition, broken hips from sudden falls is a major cause of injury for the elderly, and tai chi, which trains people to maintain a sense of balance as they shift from one form to another, helps to prevent this problem. (By the way, all of the information on tai chi's beneficial effects have been confirmed by scientific studies.)

The dual goals of tai chi is to train both the body and the mind. Tai chi teaches people to focus only on the particular position being performed at the moment. This freedom from distracting thoughts create a tranquil state of mind similar to that produced by practising meditation or yoga. This makes tai chi an especially effective form of exercise in today's high-stress society.

Unit

3

Identifying and Punctuating the Main Types of Sentences

Compound Sentences

A **compound sentence,** a very common sentence pattern, contains *at least two subjects and two verbs,* usually arranged in an S–V/S–V pattern. For example,

    S   V   S V
Bob wrecked his car last week, and now he rides the bus to work.

    S   V   S V
Nina lived in Italy for two years, so she speaks Italian fluently.

In grammar, the term **compound** means "having two or more parts." Thus, a sentence may have a **compound subject,** for example, "The *husband* and his *wife* were at the opera." Or, a sentence may have a **compound verb,** for example, "The man *rode* his bike and *sped* down the street." Do not confuse a sentence with a **compound subject** or a **compound verb** with a **compound sentence.**

A compound sentence can be divided into two parts, each of which can be a separate sentence by itself.

Bob wrecked his car last week.   +   Now he rides the bus to work.

Nina lived in Italy for two years.   +   She speaks Italian fluently.

Because a compound sentence can be divided into *two* separate sentences, each half of a compound sentence must contain at least one subject and one verb. Therefore, each half of a compound sentence is a **clause.** *A clause is a group of words that contains both a subject and a verb.* (In contrast, a group of words that does not contain both a subject and a verb is called a **phrase,** as in a prepositional phrase.) A clause that can stand alone as a complete sentence is called an **independent clause.** Because each clause in a compound sentence can stand alone as a complete sentence, each clause must be independent. In other words,

A compound sentence consists of at least two independent clauses joined together to form a single sentence.

There are two ways to join independent clauses to form a compound sentence. The most frequently used method is to put a conjunction between the clauses. *A* **conjunction** *is a word that joins words or groups of words.* In grammar, the word *coordinate* means "of equal importance." Therefore, the conjunctions that are used in compound sentences are called **coordinating conjunctions** because they join two groups of words that are of equal grammatical importance. (They are both independent clauses.) The following coordinating conjunctions are used to join the clauses of compound sentences:

and

but

for (when it means *because*)

nor

or

so

yet

You should *memorize* these coordinating conjunctions because later you will have to be able to distinguish between them and the connecting words that are used to form other kinds of sentences.

Some students use the following made-up word to help them remember coordinating conjunctions:

F	A	N	B	O	Y	S
for	and	nor	but	or	yet	so

▶ In the following sentences, underline the subjects of the compound sentences *once* and the verbs *twice,* and circle the coordinating conjunction that joins the clauses. Notice that a comma *precedes* the coordinating conjunction.

The premier entered the room, and the band began to play.

She diets constantly, but her weight remains the same.

I rarely prepare casseroles, for my family refuses to eat them.

We must hurry, or we will miss the first part of the movie.

He can't help you, nor can I.

(Notice that when the conjunction *nor* is used to join two independent clauses, the pattern becomes S–V/V–S: My coat isn't here, nor is my hat.)

The defendant was ill, so the trial was postponed.

He earns only $1,200 a month, yet he lives quite comfortably.

▶ Construct compound sentences of your own, using the coordinating conjunctions listed below to join your clauses. Underline the subject of each clause *once* and the verb *twice.* (You may construct a clause that has more than one subject and/or more than one verb, but each clause must have *at least* one subject and one verb.)

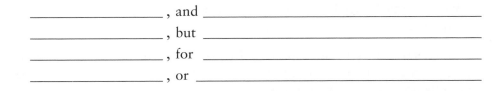

The second way to join the clauses in a compound sentence is to use a semicolon (;) *in place of both the comma and the coordinating conjunction.* For example,

She could not find her keys; they must have fallen somewhere.

Mark is always late for work; he oversleeps every morning.

Compound sentences constructed with semicolons occur less frequently than compound sentences constructed with coordinating conjunctions because some type of connecting word is usually needed to show the relationship between the clauses. For example, without a coordinating conjunction the logical relationship between the two clauses in the following sentence might be confusing.

My grandfather has lived in Canada for fifty years; he has never learned to speak English.

If, however, you replace the semicolon with a coordinating conjunction, the relationship between the clauses becomes clear.

My grandfather has lived in Canada for fifty years, but he has never learned to speak English.

It is all right to use the semicolon by itself between the clauses of a compound sentence, but do so only when the relationship between the clauses is clear without a connecting word.

▶ Construct two compound sentences of your own, using semicolons to join the clauses. Underline the subjects *once* and the verbs *twice*. Make certain that each clause has at least one subject and one verb.

_____ ; _____

_____ ; _____

Another common way to show the relationship between the clauses of a compound sentence is to use a **conjunctive adverb,** such as *however,* in the second clause. Notice that a *semicolon* is required between the clauses. A comma follows the conjunctive adverb.

We all studied quite hard; however, the test was more difficult than we had expected.

Conjunctive adverbs are especially frequent in formal language, in which expressing the precise relationship between ideas is the goal. Here are the most frequently used conjunctive adverbs:

To Add an Idea	*To Conclude*	*To Compare/Contrast*	*For Time Order*
also	consequently	however	finally
anyway	hence	instead	meanwhile
besides	therefore	likewise	next
furthermore	thus	nevertheless	still
incidentally		nonetheless	then
indeed		otherwise	
moreover			

A conjunctive adverb gets its double name from the fact that it does two things at once: It connects, like other **conjunctions,** and it modifies, like other **adverbs.** Because it is adverbial, it can be located in many places in its own clause. Because it can move around in the second clause and does not always come *exactly between* the two clauses (like coordinating conjunctions), it does not necessarily act as a signal to readers that they are coming to the second half of a compound sentence. For these reasons, the strong signal of a semicolon marks the end of the first clause.

Tarek loved to surf; therefore, he lived near the beach.

Joe, however, liked to hike; he lived near the mountains.

▶ Notice that the conjunctive adverb is always "set off" with a comma, or two commas, in its own clause. Construct three compound sentences of your own that use conjunctive adverbs. Try putting the conjunctive adverb in several different places in the second clause.

1. _____

2. _____

3. _____

(Did you remember to "set off" the conjunctive adverb with one or two commas?)

As you can see from the sentences that you have constructed in this lesson, the following punctuation rules apply to compound sentences:

1. If the clauses in a compound sentence are joined by a coordinating conjunction, place a comma *before* (to the left of) the conjunction.

This sentence is compound, and it contains a comma.

You may have learned that it is not necessary to use commas in short compound sentences (for example, "He's a Scorpio and I'm a Libra."). Although this is true, not everyone agrees on how short a "short" compound sentence is, so if you are in doubt, it is safer to use a comma. All the sentences in the exercises for this unit will be "long" compound sentences and should have a comma before the conjunction.

2. Although a compound sentence may contain more than one coordinating conjunction, the comma is placed before the conjunction that joins the clauses.

Jan and I attended the same college, and now we work for the same company.

3. If the clauses in a compound sentence are *not* joined by a coordinating conjunction, place a semicolon between the clauses. If the clauses are joined by a conjunctive adverb, the adverb must also be *followed* by a comma.

I don't have my book with me; I must have left it at home.

We hurried to the theatre; however, the film was over.

The following sentence patterns do *not* require commas because they are simple (meaning that they contain only one clause) rather than compound.

S–V–V	He ordered a baked potato but was served French fries instead. (no comma)
S–S–V	My uncle and aunt live in Boston. (no comma)
S–S–V–V	My cousin and I went to England and stayed there for two months. (no comma)

To review, the three patterns for punctuating a compound sentence are: independent clause + comma + coordinating conjunction + independent clause

We went to a play, and next we had some dinner.

independent clause + semicolon + independent clause

We didn't enjoy the movie; it was boring.

independent clause + semicolon + conjunctive adverb + comma + independent clause

I love to draw; however, I have little artistic talent.

Exercise 9A

▶ Add commas and semicolons to the following sentences wherever they are needed. If a sentence needs no additional punctuation (in other words, if the sentence is simple rather than compound), label it C for *correct*.

1. Both children and adults enjoy the story of Peter Pan for the idea of never growing up has a magical appeal.

2. James Matthew Barrie created this tale in 1904 however few people know the story behind its origin.

3. The story of Peter Pan and the life of James Barrie are linked at many levels.

4. The early death of Barrie's older brother David had a great influence on him and it may be a source for the character of Peter.

5. Barrie's mother loved David best so James lived the first six years of his life in his older brother's shadow.

6. David died at the age of fourteen James then tried to become a replacement for his dead brother.

7. David never had a chance to grow up therefore like Peter Pan, he remained a boy forever to the members of his family.

8. James also stopped growing after his brother's death and remained short for the rest of his life.

9. In 1894, Barrie married an actress named Mary Ansell however the couple had no children.

10. Barrie enjoyed the company of children thus he became attached to the five sons of his friends Sylvia and Arthur Llewelyn Davies.

11. Unfortunately, the boys' parents died subsequently Barrie became their legal guardian.

12. Barrie often told the Davies' children stories and their favourite stories were about a group of boys like them.

13. The telling of these stories gave birth to Neverland and to the character of Peter Pan.

14. Barrie also knew a young girl named Margaret Henley and she accidentally provided the name for another main character.

15. Margaret had a special name for Barrie she called him "my friendly."

16. However, Margaret lisped consequently she pronounced "friendly" as "fwendy" or "wendy."

17. Barrie's life seems to be marked by the early deaths of people close to him for Margaret died at the age of six.

18. She never lived long enough to see the publication of *Peter Pan* nevertheless her memory is preserved in the character of Wendy.

EXERCISE 9B

▶ Add commas and semicolons to the following sentences wherever they are needed. If a sentence needs no additional punctuation (in other words, if the sentence is simple rather than compound), label it C for *correct*.

1. Today's consumers take the convenience of frozen food for granted however commercially frozen food was not available until the 1930s.

2. Manufacturers had tried to freeze food before then but the finished product did not taste good.

3. Then, in the early 1900s, Clarence Birdseye went to the Canadian Arctic and discovered the secret of freezing food successfully.

4. Birdseye originally wanted to study natural sciences so he enrolled in Amherst College in Massachusetts.

5. He left college after two years for he lacked the funds to complete his education.

6. Birdseye entered the fur-trading business in 1912 and began travelling in the Canadian Arctic to collect furs to sell.

7. The Inuit of the region lived by hunting and they often used the Arctic's freezing temperatures to preserve meat for later use.

8. During winter, meat froze almost immediately however freezing took longer during the milder temperatures of autumn.

9. Frozen meat from the winter months tasted as good as fresh meat but frozen meat from the autumn months did not.

10. Food must be frozen quickly or it will form large ice crystals.

11. These large crystals damage the cell walls of the food and affect its flavour, texture, and colour.

12. Birdseye now understood the need for rapid freezing next he had to invent a machine to perform the process.

13. He invented the "Quick Freeze Machine" in 1925 and began producing frozen food for sale.

14. His products were not widely known for he lacked the funds to advertise and to sell them nationwide.

15. In 1929, Birdseye decided to sell his company and it became a part of the General Foods Corporation.

16. General Foods kept Birdseye's name but divided it into two words.

17. Frozen food was not popular during the 1930s many consumers would not buy this new product.

18. The frozen food industry might have failed however it was saved by the United States' entry into the Second World War.

19. During the war, the supply of tin was limited and the United States government restricted its use in the food canning industry.

20. Canned goods became expensive so many customers turned to frozen food.

21. Frozen food was packaged in paper boxes thus it was not affected by wartime rationing.

22. Consumers became familiar with frozen food and learned to appreciate its flavour and convenience.

23. The 1950s brought another boost to frozen food for in 1954 the Swanson Company introduced frozen TV dinners.

24. The widespread use of microwave ovens during the 1980s and 1990s made frozen food even more convenient for it was now possible to heat food in only a few minutes.

25. Today, many frozen products still bear the Birds Eye name and Clarence Birdseye is still remembered as the "father of frozen food."

Complex Sentences

There are two kinds of clauses, independent and dependent. As you have seen in Chapter 9, **independent clauses** can stand alone as complete sentences. For example,

I was ill.

We loved the play.

A **dependent clause,** however, *cannot* stand alone as a complete sentence. Instead, it must be attached to, or *depend* on, an *independent* clause to form a grammatically complete sentence and to express a complete idea. Notice that the following dependent clauses are not complete sentences.

When he comes over . . .

If we come to the play . . .

Before we saw the movie . . .

These clauses seem incomplete because they are actually only part of a sentence. Using the first of the following sentences as a model, change each dependent clause into a complete sentence by adding an appropriate *independent* clause.

When he comes over, *we watch television.*

If we come to the play, _____

Before we saw the movie, _____

You have now constructed two complex sentences. A **complex sentence** contains both independent and dependent clauses. (In contrast, a **compound sentence** contains only *independent* clauses.)

Every dependent clause begins with a subordinating conjunction. A **conjunction** joins words or groups of words. The conjunctions that begin dependent clauses are called **subordinating conjunctions** because the word *subordinate* means "of lesser importance." Grammatically speaking, a dependent clause is "less important" than an independent clause because it cannot stand alone as a complete sentence. In contrast, the conjunctions that you used in the previous chapter to form compound sentences are called **coordinating conjunctions** because *coordinate* means "of equal importance." Because both of the clauses in a compound sentence are independent, both clauses are "of equal importance."

The type of dependent clause that you will be studying in this chapter is called an **adverb clause** because, like other adverbs, an adverb clause describes a verb (or sometimes an adjective or an adverb). It is the same kind of clause that you worked with in Chapter 2. The subordinating conjunctions used to begin adverb clauses describe verbs by telling *how, when, where, why,* or *under what conditions* the action occurs.

how: as if, as though

when: after, as, as soon as, before, until, when, whenever, while

where: where, wherever

why: because, in order that, since, so that

under what conditions: although, as long as, even though, if, though, unless

▶ Read the following sentences. A slanted line indicates the point at which each sentence divides into two separate clauses. Underline the subject of each clause *once* and the verb *twice*. Circle the subordinating conjunction.

While we studied, / he watched television.

I babysat / so that they could go to a movie.

As long as we communicate, / we will remain friends.

Now examine the clause in each sentence that contains the circled subordinating conjunction.

The clause that contains the subordinating conjunction is the dependent clause.

Notice that in a complex sentence, the dependent clause may be either the first or the second clause in the sentence.

When Todd wants to relax, he goes fishing.

Enrico finds time to exercise *after he finishes work.*

In most cases, the adverb clauses in a complex sentence are *reversible.* That is, the sentence has the same basic meaning no matter which clause comes first. For example,

While he is on the train, he usually reads his books.

He usually reads his books *while he is on the train.*

or

If we go on vacation, we will have lots of fun.

We will have lots of fun *if we go on vacation.*

However, *the order* of the clauses in a complex sentence *does affect the punctuation* of the sentence.

1. If the **dependent** clause is the first clause in the sentence, it is followed by a comma.

   Before she performed at the club, Stephanie welcomed her guests.

2. If the **independent** clause is the first clause in the sentence, no comma is needed.

   Stephanie welcomed her guests *before she performed at the club.*

▶   Punctuate the following complex sentences. First circle the subordinating conjunction in each sentence, and draw a slanted line between the clauses.

After we eat dinner we're going to see a movie.

The child carries her teddy bear with her wherever she goes.

If it doesn't rain the crops will be ruined.

As soon as I finish painting my apartment I'll help you paint yours.

Exercise 10A

▶ The following sentences are **complex.** First, underline the dependent clause in each sentence. Then add a comma to the sentence if it is necessary. If a sentence needs no additional punctuation, label it C for *correct.*

1. Although most of us think there is only one Peter Pan story there are actually many versions.

2. Barrie originally wrote the story of Peter Pan as a series of skits so that the sons of the Llewelyn Davies could perform in them.

3. Peter Pan first appeared in print in a 1902 novel by Barrie where he is introduced in one of the novel's episodes.

4. After the novel was published Barrie used this episode as a source for his 1904 play *Peter Pan, or The Boy Who Wouldn't Grow Up.*

5. Because the play was so successful Barrie turned his character of Peter Pan into a 1906 book titled *Peter Pan in Kensington Gardens.*

6. As if Barrie wanted to confuse us with all his Peter Pan versions in 1911 he wrote a second novel based on the play, *Peter and Wendy.*

▶ Sentences 7–15 are a mixture of **compound** and **complex** sentences. Add commas and semicolons to the sentences wherever they are needed. If a sentence needs no additional punctuation, label it C for *correct.*

7. Because Barrie's play needed flying characters and other elaborate technical requirements it was originally rejected by theatre producers.

8. In its first production, the lead of Peter Pan was performed by a thirty-seven-year-old woman and many women have played Peter since then.

9. The role of Peter Pan was played by a woman in the United States from 1905 to 1915 but Barrie never had the chance to see any of the American productions.

10. Peter Pan has been played by other famous American actresses they include Mary Martin (1954), Sandy Duncan (1979–1980), and Cathy Rigby (1990–1991).

11. Because Peter Foy invented the "Floating Pulley" and the "Track-on Track" systems all of these actresses were able to fly across the stage.

12. Even though there have been many memorable female Peter Pans some males have also starred in this role.

13. Disney's animated film features a male Peter and Robin Williams played a grown-up Peter in the movie *Hook*.

14. The most recent Peter Pan movie was released in December, 2003 it also has a male main character, played by Jeremy Sumpter.

15. Apparently, the magic of Peter Pan remains whether a female or male performs the role.

EXERCISE 10B

▶ The following exercise includes simple, compound, and complex sentences. Add commas and semicolons wherever they are needed. If a sentence is simple and needs no additional punctuation, label it C for *correct*.

1. When environmentalists think of the year 2005 they recall the most severe storms and hottest temperatures in recorded history.

2. That year also recorded the most Arctic ice melting and the worst Atlantic hurricane season indicating the serious climate change that scientists had been warning us about.

3. Many weather-related disasters are natural events but are these becoming more frequent and more severe as a result of human behaviour?

4. The world experienced the devastating Asian Tsunami in December of 2004 Hurricanes Rita and Katrina swept along the American southeast coast in the summer of 2005 and a huge earthquake struck in the Himalayas in Pakistan a few months later.

5. When gases like carbon monoxide get into the atmosphere whether from natural causes industry or autos they are trapped and create what is called the greenhouse effect.

6. Earth's natural greenhouse effect allows us to live on the planet without freezing however too many gases trap the heat and cause global warming.

7. Global warming is an ongoing and natural event global warming with this rapid increase in temperature is a threat to our planet.

8. Governments and scientists around the world met under the United Nations to work out ways to reduce the speed of the planet's warming.

9. They agreed to find ways to cut greenhouse gas emissions and to do it within a limited time frame.

10. The agreement, called the Kyoto Protocol, aims to encourage nations to reduce their pollution therefore reducing the amount of such gas in the atmosphere.

11. Before industrialization brought the need to burn so much fossil fuel people lived in closer balance with nature.

12. Now it will take a huge effort in the developed and developing countries to cut greenhouse gas emissions furthermore it will cost a great deal of money.

13. Global warming results in glacial ice melting and this in turn leads to a rising sea level which could put coastal regions underwater.

14. Because of a warmer atmosphere the rate at which the sea is rising has increased much more quickly than was predicted.

15. This effect also changes the amounts of rainfall and the ocean currents resulting in increased flooding and hurricanes.

16. Nevertheless, there is something each of us can do to reduce greenhouse gases and that is cut back on our energy use.

17. When we use an electrical appliance we are using energy that is usually produced by burning fossil fuels.

18. By turning off appliances not in use and turning down the thermostat or purchasing only energy-saving devices we can help reduce global warming.

19. Recycling saves energy used in manufacturing and in garbage disposal so is also an effective way to help.

20. In addition, we can all try to limit our auto emissions by keeping our cars tuned up not idling or, better yet, carpooling or using public transit.

21. If scientists continue to develop alternative energy sources such as solar and wind power and international governments work together then there is hope that the rate of global warming can be reduced.

Avoiding Run-On Sentences and Comma Splices

As you learned in Chapter 9, a compound sentence consists of at least two independent clauses. The independent clauses in a compound sentence must be separated either by a coordinating conjunction (such as *and, but, or*) preceded by a comma or by a semicolon if no conjunction is used.

*Failure to separate two independent clauses results in an error known as a **run-on sentence.*** The following are examples of run-on sentences:

I don't play tennis well I have a poor backhand.

The next game is at our school we want to go to it.

Run-on sentences are very serious errors. They are not only confusing to the reader but also indicate that the writer cannot tell where one sentence ends and another begins.

There are three ways to correct a run-on sentence.

1. Divide the run-on into two separate sentences, ending each with a period. (If the sentences are questions, end them with question marks.)

I don't play tennis well. I have a poor backhand.

The next game is at our school. We want to go to it.

Although this method produces grammatically correct sentences, an essay written completely in such short, simple sentences creates the choppy effect of an elementary school reading text. Therefore, you should also consider using the two other methods of correcting run-ons.

2. Change the run-on to a **compound sentence** by separating the clauses with a coordinating conjunction, a conjunctive adverb, or just a semicolon if the relationship between the clauses is clear without a conjunction.

I don't play tennis well, *for* I have a poor backhand.

or

I have a poor backhand; *as a result,* I don't play tennis well.

or

I don't play tennis well; I have a poor backhand.

The next game is at our school, *so* we want to go to it.

or

The next game is at our school; *therefore,* we want to go to it.

or

The next game is at our school; we want to go to it.

As you learned previously, the relationship between the two clauses in a compound sentence is often clearer if a conjunction is used rather than a semicolon.

3. Change the run-on to a complex sentence by placing a subordinating conjunction before one of the clauses.

I don't play tennis well *because* I have a poor backhand.

Because the next game is at our school, we want to go to it.

Another very common error is the comma splice. Unlike a run-on, in which two independent clauses are run together with no punctuation, a **comma splice** consists of two independent clauses joined with *not enough* punctuation—that is, with only a comma (and *no* coordinating conjunction). The following are examples of comma splices:

Kari is a full-time student, she works forty hours a week.

Jason needs a new car, he can't afford to buy one now.

A comma by itself is *not* a strong enough punctuation mark to separate two independent clauses. Only periods and semicolons can be used without conjunctions to separate independent clauses. Comma splices can be corrected by the same three methods used for correcting run-on sentences.

1. Divide the comma splice into two separate sentences.

   Kari is a full-time student. She works forty hours a week.

   Jason needs a new car. He can't afford to buy one now.

2. Change the comma splice into a **compound sentence** by separating the clauses with either a coordinating conjunction, conjunctive adverb, or just a semicolon if the relationship between the two clauses is clear without a conjunction.

   Kari is a full-time student, *and* she works forty hours a week.

   or

   Kari is a full-time student; *in addition,* she works forty hours a week.

   Jason needs a new car, *but* he can't afford to buy one now.

   or

   Jason needs a new car; *however,* he can't afford to buy one now.

3. Change the comma splice into a **complex sentence** by placing a subordinating conjunction before one of the clauses.

   Even though Kari is a full-time student, she works forty hours a week.

   Although Jason needs a new car, he can't afford to buy one now.

Remember that if the dependent clause (the clause continuing the subordinating conjunction) is the first clause in the sentence, it should be followed by a comma.

▶ Correct the following run-on sentences and comma splices:

I would like to visit New Brunswick I have many relatives there.

All my sisters have blue eyes I do not.

Gary grew up in Whitehorse, he is used to cold weather.

They are always in debt they have too many credit cards.

EXERCISE 11A

▶ Correct all the run-on sentences and comma splices. Try to use as many different conjunctions as possible. If a sentence is neither a run-on nor a comma splice, label it C for *correct*.

1. Computers make it possible to transmit information rapidly from one place to another, it is no longer necessary for employees working on the same project to be in the same place.

2. For many people, the most convenient place to work is at home this eliminates having to commute to a workplace.

3. These "telecommuters" are growing in number, they are still a small (less than 10 percent) proportion of Canadian employees.

4. There are many benefits to working at home, but there are also major disadvantages.

5. People have to travel a long distance to their offices, the time saved by working at home can significantly shorten their working day. (Try using the conjunction *if.*)

6. Drivers save money on gasoline and car insurance, some families may no longer even need a second car.

7. Telecommuters also save money on clothes they don't have to purchase special outfits to wear to work.

8. Furthermore, they control their own time, they can determine their own work schedules.

9. They don't have to begin work at a specific time, they don't have to work for a fixed number of hours. (Try using the conjunction *nor.*)

10. However, there are also disadvantages to working at home one of the greatest is being separated from other employees.

11. Many people enjoy the companionship of their coworkers they feel lonely and isolated at home.

12. They may even have fewer chances to be promoted, their bosses rarely talk to them or observe them working.

13. The old saying "out of sight, out of mind" is often true working at home may not be the best career move.

14. Another big problem is coping with distractions employees working at home may be interrupted by children or other family members.

15. Employees in an office can temporarily forget about unfinished chores at home, such as paying bills or doing housework, telecommuters find it more difficult to separate their home and work lives.

16. Working at home usually saves money there are some extra expenses.

17. Most telecommuters set aside a separate room in their homes to use as an office, they may also have to purchase office equipment, like a fax machine or a high-quality printer.

18. Working at home certainly has advantages it is definitely not for everyone.

Exercise 11B

▶ The following essay contains run-on sentences and comma splices. Correct these errors using the methods you have learned from this and previous lessons.

Anniversary celebrations for people are routine events, an anniversary party for a book is a more unusual occurrence. In the summer of 2004, thousands of people gathered in Dublin, Ireland, they wanted to honour the most famous novel by Ireland's most famous author. The author was James Joyce the novel was *Ulysses*. *Ulysses* was actually published in 1922 however all the events in this very long novel take place in Dublin on June 16, 1904. Dublin celebrates June 16th of every year as a holiday 2004's 100th anniversary was the biggest celebration of all.

Some people may consider this a bad pun the celebration's official name was the ReJoyce festival. A main feature of the festival was guided tours of Dublin these tours followed the route taken by Leopold Bloom, the novel's main character. Many visitors stopped for a drink at the Davy Byrnes pub. The pub is famous, both Leopold Bloom and Joyce himself frequented this bar. To honour the occasion, the pub served a special lunch of a Gorgonzola cheese sandwich and a glass of burgundy wine this was the lunch Leopold Bloom ordered in the novel. A more formal event re-created Bloom's breakfast. The city converted a main thoroughfare into a turn-of-the-century marketplace it served Bloom's breakfast of kidney and Guinness ale to almost ten thousand people there. Many guests wore 1904 costumes to the breakfast competitions were held to choose people most closely resembling the novel's main characters.

The festival also included more traditional literary events. Dublin hosted the 19th International James Joyce Symposium. This academic conference offered a week of lectures, workshops, and performances it attracted scholars from all over the world. Ireland's National Library had a special exhibit on James Joyce and *Ulysses* other museums had exhibits of art inspired by Joyce's works.

Ulysses is a long and very complex work in fact many more people begin the book than actually finish it. The festival's organizers wanted their events to make the novel more accessible they also encouraged the public to listen to the book on audiotape or to read it in book clubs. Even the festival's official website was designed to encourage people to read *Ulysses,* it included background material on Joyce and his works and a chapter-by-chapter summary of the novel.

Correcting Fragments

The basic unit of expression in written English is the sentence. As you already know, *a sentence must contain at least one independent clause.* If you take a group of words that is *not* a complete sentence and punctuate it as though it were a complete sentence, you have created a **sentence fragment.** In other words, you have written only a piece—a fragment—of a sentence rather than a complete sentence.

As you can see. These groups of words. Are fragments.

Because semicolons and periods are usually interchangeable, fragments may also be created by misusing semicolons. If you look carefully at the following two groups of words, you will see that they should form a single complex sentence that needs only a comma, and not a semicolon.

As you can see; wrong punctuation may be confusing.

As you can see, wrong punctuation may be confusing.

Although fragments occur frequently in speech and occasionally in informal writing, they are generally not acceptable in classroom writing and should be avoided in formal writing situations.

There are two types of fragments: **dependent clauses** and **phrases.** As you have already learned in Chapter 10, a dependent clause cannot stand alone as a complete sentence. It must be attached to an independent clause to form a complex sentence.

Any dependent clause that is separated from its main clause by a period or semicolon is a fragment.

Below are several examples of this type of fragment.

When we arrived at the theatre. The movie had already begun.

When we arrived at the theatre; the movie had already begun.

We'll miss our plane. If we don't hurry.

We'll miss our plane; if we don't hurry.

▶   Eliminate the dependent clause fragments in the following paragraph by punctuating them correctly.

> Because we are trying to eat more healthful food. We are buying more fruits and vegetables. The problem occurs. Whenever we go to a restaurant. At the restaurant, desserts tempt us; although we have the best of intentions to eat only healthful foods. If we were at home; we would never think of eating pies and ice cream. Because the menu is so intriguing. We wind up ordering things no one would consider to be healthy. When we order banana splits and ice cream; it isn't healthy, but we sure are happy.

If you read the passage backwards, that is, read the last sentence first, you will spot a fragment easily.

Are you remembering to punctuate each dependent clause according to its location? As you learned in Chapter 10, if the *dependent* clause is the first clause in a sentence, it should be followed by a comma. If the *independent* clause is the first clause in a sentence, no comma is needed.

The second type of fragment is the **phrase.** Because a phrase is defined as a group of words that does not contain both a subject and a verb, a phrase obviously cannot be a complete sentence. *All phrases are fragments.* Study the following types of fragments, and notice the way each phrase has been changed from a fragment into a complete sentence.

FRAGMENT—NO SUBJECT	Had seen that film.
SENTENCE	*We* had seen that film.
FRAGMENT—NO VERB	The children on the bus.
SENTENCE	The children *rode* on the bus.
FRAGMENT—INCOMPLETE VERB (-*ING* FORM)	Kevin attending a conference.
SENTENCE	Kevin *was attending* a conference.

(An -*ing* main verb must be preceded by a helping verb.)

or

Kevin *attended* a conference.

(Change the -*ing* verb to a main verb.)

FRAGMENT—INCOMPLETE VERB (PAST PARTICIPLE)	The garden filled with flowers.
SENTENCE	The garden *is filled* with flowers.

(To be a main verb, a past participle must be preceded by a helping verb. See Chapter 25 for an explanation and a list of past participles.)

FRAGMENT—INFINITIVE	To do well in school.
SENTENCE	*Students must study* hard to do well in school.
FRAGMENT—PARTICIPIAL PHRASE	Being a good friend.
SENTENCE	Being a good friend *takes* a lot of hard work.

▶ The following groups of words are fragments because they lack either a subject or a verb or because they have an incomplete verb. Rewrite each fragment so that it becomes a complete sentence.

The weather being much too cold for swimming.

Ate a pizza for lunch yesterday.

Praying for a good turnout.

The candidate knowing that his lead would not hold.

A present sent by air mail.

The house damaged by the tornado.

The city's new subway system.

When you are writing a composition, be careful not to separate a phrase from the rest of the sentence to which it belongs.

INCORRECT	I'm looking for a small puppy. With floppy white ears.
CORRECT	I'm looking for a small puppy with floppy white ears.
INCORRECT	Wanting to do well; he studied all night.
CORRECT	Wanting to do well, he studied all night.

▶   Rewrite the following items so that any fragments are correctly joined with the sentences to which they belong.

I burned my hand. While frying chicken for dinner.

Pleased with the pianist's performance. The audience demanded an encore.

Susan lay sleeping on the beach. From noon until three o'clock.

To summarize: **Phrases** are sentence fragments because they do not contain both a subject and a complete verb. (In other words, they are not **clauses.**) **Dependent clauses** are fragments because they are not *independent* clauses. This is simply another way of stating the most basic rule of sentence construction:

Every sentence must contain at least one independent clause.

Exercise 12A

▶ Correct any fragments you find in the following exercise. If an item contains no fragments, label it C for *correct*.

1. Although the famous aviator Amelia Earhart vanished on July 2, 1937. The mystery surrounding her disappearance continues to interest people.

2. While flying around the globe at the equator. Earhart simply vanished and was never heard of again.

3. The official explanation for her death stating that her plane ran out of gas and went down in the Pacific Ocean.

4. Both Earhart and her navigator were killed in the resulting crash.

5. However, many conspiratorial theories about Earhart's death exist. Because some people are unwilling to accept the official version.

6. After thirty-two years of research. A retired Air Force colonel named Rollin C. Reineck believes he has found the answer to this mystery.

7. Reineck has a theory. Connected to actions by the United States government in the years before the Second World War began.

8. According to this theory, the American government sent Earhart on a secret spy mission. For it needed to know what the Japanese were doing in the Pacific.

9. After crash landing in the Marshall Islands; Earhart was captured by the Japanese.

10. The American government persuaded the Japanese to release Earhart and secretly brought her back to the United States.

11. Earhart was then given the assumed identity of Irene Bolam. So that no one would know she had been working as an American spy.

12. Much of Reineck's work based on the research of a man named Joe Gervais.

13. After meeting Irene Bolam in 1965. Gervais noticed a striking resemblance between her and Earhart.

14. In addition, Bolam was wearing a medallion. Resembling one awarded to Earhart by President Herbert Hoover many years earlier.

15. Reineck used a computer to age Earhart's photos from the 1930s. In order to show how much an older Earhart would resemble Irene Bolam.

16. However, no one knows for sure if Bolam was really Earhart. Because Bolam refused to allow anyone to examine her fingerprints during her lifetime.

17. Rather than having her body buried after her death in 1982. Bolam donated it for scientific research.

18. Stating, however, that her body must never be fingerprinted.

19. Her corpse was ultimately cremated. And the ashes buried in an unmarked grave.

20. If Bolam was really Amelia Earhart. She took her secret with her to her grave.

EXERCISE 12B

▶ Correct any fragments that you find in the following essay. If you underline the subject once and the verb twice as in earlier exercises, and circle coordinating conjunctions, you will easily identify fragments.

Popcorn, one of our oldest foods. Its history in North America dating back more than five thousand years.

The Indigenous Peoples having different methods for popping corn. Some tribes threw the corn on hot stones. And made a game of catching the popped kernels. While other tribes used pottery containers placed over a fire or filled with hot sand. Oil was sometimes added. To give extra flavour to the popcorn.

Popcorn sometimes used for purposes other than eating. In 1492, Columbus saw West Indian natives wearing popcorn corsages. And decorating their headdresses with popcorn. The Aztecs of Mexico even decorating statues of their gods with popcorn jewellery.

When the Pilgrims had their first Thanksgiving dinner in Plymouth, Massachusetts; the local people brought sacks of popcorn as a goodwill gift. After becoming familiar with popcorn. The colonists soon making it a part of their regular diet. They even served it with milk as a breakfast cereal. In later years, popcorn was often sweetened with molasses and made into popcorn balls.

Throughout the 18th and 19th centuries. Popcorn served in parks and at fairs and carnivals. After the introduction of films in the early 20th century. Eating popcorn became associated with seeing movies.

Popcorn became especially popular during the Great Depression of the 1930s. Because it was an inexpensive snack and one of the few affordable treats. During the early 1940s, wartime rationing limited the supply of sugar. This making candy scarce and expensive. The public soon learned to compensate. By eating three times as much popcorn as in pre-war years.

Today, microwave popcorn providing a convenient way to prepare this snack at home. Although it is difficult to believe. The average Canadian consumes almost 80 litres of popcorn a year.

Unit 3 Review

▶ Correct any run-on sentences, comma splices, or fragments in the following essay.

If you enjoy visiting distant, unfamiliar places. You should consider vacationing in the eastern Canadian Arctic. The official name for this region is Nunavut it means "our land" in the Inuit language.

Nunavut is a vast, sparsely populated land. It covers two million square kilometres of Canada including Hudson's Bay. Reaching even to the North Pole. Although it covers such a huge land and water area. Nunavut has only thirty thousand people. The youngest population in Canada. About 85 percent of the population is Inuit. Their traditional knowledge and values, known as *Inuit Qaujimatuqangit,* shaping government and business decisions.

Due to long distances between communities. Transportation is by plane or sealift, snowmobiles are used within a community. The economy is growing fisheries, mineral exploration for gold and diamonds, oil and gas reserves all hold promise for further development.

The beauty of National and Territorial parks, which are home to many Arctic animals including caribou, muskox, seals, polar and grizzly bears, and whales. Attracts many visitors from all over the world. To see these animals in the wild and to photograph them. Nunavut is also a fishing paradise. Although fish grow slowly in the Arctic's cold waters. They also become much larger than their relatives in milder climates. You can try kayaking in the ocean or whitewater rafting on the region's scenic rivers. If you like boating.

Tourists are drawn to the North for its unique qualities. In the winter, tourists can see the aurora borealis (northern lights) in spring there are visits to villages for community festivals. Celebrating the age-old traditions. Visiting the villages during a festival gives tourists the chance to sample Inuit life. By building igloos, travelling by dogsled, and eating whaleskin snacks. Many people visit Cape Dorset, this village is famous for its sculpture and print-making. Artists in Pangnirtung have received worldwide recognition for their tapestries and weaving, filmmakers recently produced the acclaimed film *Atanarjuat—The Fast Runner.* Young people developing media and broadcast skills.

Despite the highest cost of living in Canada and working with four languages. Nunavut has established its own law school a Teacher Education Program and a Nursing Program. Linking to other universities using electronic communications.

Visitors travelling through Nunavut on their own needing to take special precautions. They must register with the nearest Royal Canadian Mounted Police station. Before they enter a wilderness area. And check in again when they return. Campers are reminded not to feed any wildlife. They must be especially careful around bears. By storing food and cooking utensils at least two hundred metres away from their tents. Protective clothing and insect repellant are also important the Arctic can be full of mosquitoes during summertime.

If your idea of a good vacation includes seeing beautiful scenery, enjoying new cultural experiences, and being far away from crowded urban areas. Then a trip to Nunavut could be in your future.

Unit 4

Punctuation That "Sets Off" or Separates

Chapter 13

Parenthetical Expressions

When speaking, people often interrupt their sentences with expressions such as *by the way, after all,* or as *a matter of fact.* These expressions are not really part of the main idea of the sentence; instead, they are interrupting—or **parenthetical**—expressions. In speech, people indicate that these parenthetical expressions are not part of the main idea of the sentence by pausing and dropping their voices before and after the expression. In writing, the same pauses are indicated with commas.

You have already learned that commas may be used to separate the clauses in compound and complex sentences. Another major function of the comma is to "set off" interrupting or **parenthetical expressions** from the rest of the sentence in which they occur.

Read the following sentences aloud, and notice how the commas around the italicized parenthetical expressions correspond to the pauses you make in speech.

Well, I guess I have to leave now.

She's only a child, *after all*.

Did you know, *by the way*, that we're getting a new boss?

The rule for punctuating parenthetical expressions is very simple:

A parenthetical expression must be completely set off from the rest of the sentence by commas.

This means that if the parenthetical expression occurs at the *beginning* of the sentence, it is *followed* by a comma. For example,

No, I don't know where they keep their knives.

If the parenthetical expression is at the *end* of the sentence, it is *preceded* by a comma.

The winner of the contest was Shani, *not Kamran*.

If the parenthetical expression is in the *middle* of the sentence, it is both *preceded* and *followed* by a comma.

Some seafood, *especially swordfish and tilefish*, may contain harmful amounts of mercury.

There are many parenthetical expressions. Some of the most frequently used ones are listed below:

after all
as a matter of fact
at any rate
etc. (an abbreviation of the Latin words *et cetera*, meaning "and other things")
for example
for instance
furthermore
however
in fact
nevertheless
of course
on the other hand
on the whole
therefore

well (at the beginning of a sentence)

yes and *no* (at the beginning of a sentence)

Expressions such as the following are often parenthetical if they occur in a position *other than* at the beginning of a sentence:

does it

doesn't it

I believe

I suppose

I hope

I think

is it

isn't it

that is

you know

For example,

He won the election, I believe.

Smoking, you know, is bad for your health.

Continual repetition of the parenthetical expression *you know* should be avoided in both speech and writing. If you are speaking clearly and your listener is paying attention, he or she knows what you are saying and does not have to be constantly reminded of the fact. Besides, you know, continually repeating *you know* can be irritating to your listener, and, you know, it doesn't really accomplish anything.

Study the following points carefully.

1. Some of the above words and phrases can be either parenthetical or not parenthetical, depending on how they are used in a sentence.

If an expression is parenthetical, it can be removed from the sentence, and what remains will still be a complete sentence.

PARENTHETICAL   The problems, *after all,* are difficult.

NOT PARENTHETICAL   He left *after all* the work was done.

PARENTHETICAL   There is a football game today, *I believe.*

NOT PARENTHETICAL   *I believe* what you tell me.

2. Because the abbreviation *etc.* is parenthetical, it must be *preceded* and *followed* by a comma if it occurs in the middle of a sentence.

Books, stationery, art supplies, *etc.,* are sold at the corner store.

The final comma after *etc.* indicates that *etc.* is parenthetical. Notice that this comma serves a different function from the commas that separate the items in the series. (The period is part of the abbreviation.)

3. **Conjunctive adverbs,** like *however* and *nevertheless,* are considered parenthetical and are set off from the clause in which they occur. They should be punctuated in simple sentences as follows:

I thought the plan was a secret. *However,* everyone seems to know about it.

or

I thought the plan was a secret. Everyone, *however,* seems to know about it.

In the second clause of a compound sentence, **conjunctive adverbs** should be punctuated as follows:

She earns a good salary; *nevertheless,* she always seems to be borrowing money from her friends.

The concert was long; *however,* it was quite beautiful.

The semicolon is needed because the clauses in the compound sentence are not joined by a coordinating conjunction. The semicolon also takes the place of the comma that would normally precede a parenthetical expression occurring in the middle of a sentence. A comma follows the parenthetical expression to set it off from the remainder of the sentence.

4. People's names and titles are also set off by commas *if you are speaking directly to them* in a sentence. This type of construction is called **direct address.** The punctuation of direct address is the same as that used for parenthetical expressions.

Have you played your guitar today, *Kwame?*

Ladies and gentlemen, please be seated.

Notice that names and titles are set off by commas only when the person is being *directly addressed* in the sentence. Otherwise, no commas are needed.

Music has always been important to Kwame. (no commas)

Kwame, have you always loved music? (comma for direct address)

EXERCISE 13A

▶ Add commas and semicolons to the following sentences wherever they are needed. If a sentence needs no additional punctuation, label it C for *correct*. This exercise deals only with the punctuation rules in Chapter 13.

1. A great many animals are I believe in need of protection.

2. These animals are near extinction and therefore deserve our attention.

3. For example the grizzly bear, the mountain lion, the condor, and eagle are familiar protected species.

4. Few of us however are aware of the plight of the orangutans.

5. Orangutans are in fact also an endangered species.

6. I suppose few people know that their native habitat is on only two islands, Borneo and Sumatra.

7. Moreover the number of orangutans on these islands is steadily decreasing.

8. You I'm sure have probably guessed the reason for their declining numbers.

9. The orangutans' habitat is being destroyed by commercial activities for instance farming and logging.

10. In addition hunters try to capture baby orangutans in order to sell them illegally as pets.

11. Hunters usually kill the baby orangutan's mother to prevent her from interfering in the capture of her infant therefore this reduces the number of orangutans born in the future.

12. Baby orangutans are exceptionally cute animals however they soon grow to a size and strength that makes keeping them at home impossible.

13. Consequently many captive orangutans are abandoned and will die if they are not rescued by wildlife organizations.

14. Wildlife organizations can train young orangutans to live in the wild again however adult apes may spend the rest of their lives at rescue centres.

15. Orangutans are very intelligent in fact they have been observed using tools.

16. For example orangutans use large leaves as umbrellas to protect themselves from the rain, and they use small folded leaves as cups for drinking water.

17. They are so intelligent in fact that scientists are trying to teach these apes to use language by pointing to symbols for words on a computer screen.

18. It seems that many people have become aware of the orangutans' plight, for websites list a dozen or more organizations working to preserve and to rescue these animals.

19. It would be tragic wouldn't it if this and other endangered species were to vanish from the Earth.

EXERCISE 13B

▶ Add commas and semicolons to the following essay wherever they are necessary. This exercise requires adding punctuation only for parenthetical expressions.

If people are asked to name the human body's largest organ, they usually choose an internal organ for example the lungs or the stomach. Nevertheless the correct answer is the skin. The skin of an average-size adult male covers an area of more than 1.85 square metres. This is a surprising statistic isn't it? The most obvious function of the skin is to provide a protective barrier between our internal organs and the outside environment. However the skin also performs other important functions essential to the body's survival.

One important function of the skin is to regulate the body's temperature. When the body becomes overheated, the skin begins to sweat. Sweating cools the body through evaporation. It is therefore a kind of internal air conditioning system. In contrast when the skin reacts to cold temperatures, the body begins to shiver. The muscle activity of shivering raises the body's temperature and makes it feel warmer.

Skin also provides us with our sense of touch. Touch is one of our most important senses in fact it is crucial to normal human development. Humans can develop normally even if they lack one of the other basic senses for example vision or hearing, but they will not develop normally if they do not receive enough touching.

In the 1960s, a scientist used monkeys to perform an experiment on keeping infants from being touched. The baby monkeys were allowed to see and hear their mothers however they were prevented from touching them. The baby monkeys soon showed signs of severe emotional distress. For instance they cried for hours at a time or rocked back and forth with their hands covering their faces. The monkeys had sufficient food and water nevertheless they failed to thrive and develop normally. The scientist used monkeys for this experiment because of course it would have been unethical to try this experiment on human infants. Now however it is also considered inhumane to subject animals to this kind of treatment.

On the other hand as a result of this kind of experiment, people began to realize the importance of touch in human development. For example like the monkeys in the experiment, infants confined in hospitals for long periods of time sometimes suffered the same kind of emotional harm. Therefore many hospitals now use volunteers to hold babies and stimulate their sense of touch.

Even touching animals can be beneficial. Experiments have shown that stroking a pet for instance a dog or cat, can make ill patients more relaxed and reduce high blood pressure. Therefore some hospitals and nursing homes are now visited by animals trained to interact with ill people.

Furthermore touching even an inanimate object may also be comforting. We have all seen babies and young children clutching favourite blankets and fuzzy toys haven't we?

It is no wonder therefore that humans can survive without some of their internal organs however they cannot survive without their skin.

Appositives

In your writing, you sometimes use a noun whose meaning may not be as clear to your reader as it is to you. For example, suppose that you write:

Mr. Singh needs to sign these forms.

If you think that your reader may not know who Mr. Singh is, you can add a phrase to your sentence to provide more information about him.

Mr. Singh, *the director of the Department of Financial Aid,* needs to sign these forms.

This kind of explanatory phrase is called an **appositive** (from the verb to *appose,* meaning "to place things beside each other"). An appositive is a phrase placed beside a noun to clarify that noun's meaning. Study the following sentences, in which the appositives have been italicized. Notice that each appositive *immediately follows the noun it describes.*

July, *the seventh month in our calendar,* was named after Julius Caesar.

The impact of the earthquake destroyed complete villages in the Himalayas, *the rugged mountains of Kashmir,* a region disputed by India and Pakistan.

Poi, *the staple food of the Hawaiian diet,* is made from taro root.

As you can see, appositives must be set off by commas from the rest of the sentence just as parenthetical expressions are. Appositives are considered *extra* elements in a sentence because they add additional information about a noun that has already been *specifically identified.* For example, in the sentence about *July* above, even without the appositive "the seventh month in our calendar," you know which month was named after Julius Caesar because the month has been specifically identified as *July.* In the next example, even without the appositive "the rugged mountains of Kashmir," you know that the earthquake that destroyed villages was in the *Himalayas.* In the third example, even without the appositive "the staple food of the Hawaiian diet," the food is specifically identified as *poi.*

Here is the rule for punctuating this kind of explanatory phrase or clause:

If a phrase or clause adds additional information about a noun that has already been specifically identified, that phrase or clause must be completely set off from the rest of the sentence by commas.

In this lesson, you will be dealing with appositives, which are phrases. In Chapter 15, you will be applying the same rule to clauses.

Specifically identified includes mentioning either a person's first or last name, or both, or using words such as "my oldest brother," "my ten o'clock class on Monday," or "my hometown." The nouns in the last three phrases are considered to be *specifically identified* because even though you have not mentioned your brother's name, you can have only one "oldest" brother. Similarly, only one specific class can be your "ten o'clock class on Monday," and only one specific town can be your "hometown." In other words, *specifically identified* means limiting the meaning of a general word like *town* to *one particular town* or limiting a general word like *class* to *one particular class.*

▶   Underline the appositives in the following sentences, and then punctuate them. Remember that appositives *follow* the nouns that they describe.

My father a doctor at Sick Children's Hospital is attending a medical convention in San Francisco.

My twelve o'clock class on Tuesday English 110 concentrates on writing.

This summer I'm going to visit my hometown Saskatoon, Saskatchewan.

Our family will attend Pioneer Days our town's annual summer festival.

On the other hand, if a phrase is necessary to establish the specific identity of a noun, it is *not set off* by commas. Study the difference between the following two sentences.

The novel *Great Expectations* is considered by many critics to be Charles Dickens's greatest work. (No commas are used to set off *Great Expectations* because the title is necessary to identify which of Dickens's many novels is considered to be his greatest work.)

Charles Dickens's fourteenth novel, *Great Expectations,* is considered by many critics to be his greatest work. (Commas are used to set off *Great Expectations* because Dickens's greatest work has already been specifically identified as his *fourteenth* novel.)

Most single-word appositives are necessary to establish the specific identity of the nouns they follow and are, therefore, *not* set off by commas.

The color *yellow* is my favourite.

My sister *Susan* lives in Oakville.

The word *penurious* means "stingy."

► Underline the appositives in the following sentences, and then add commas wherever they are necessary. Some sentences may not require commas.

Fiat automobiles are manufactured in Turin a city in northeastern Italy.

The komodor a Hungarian sheepdog has a coat that looks like a mop.

Balboa a sixteenth-century Spanish explorer was the first European to discover the American side of the Pacific Ocean.

In the United States, fruits and vegetables are usually sold by the pound an amount equal to .45 kilograms.

Xiaolin's husband an orthopedic surgeon spends much of his time working on injured athletes.

Have you seen the movie *Titanic?*

EXERCISE 14A

▶ Add commas to the following sentences wherever they are necessary. If a sentence needs no additional punctuation, label it C for *correct*. This exercise covers only the rules from Chapter 14.

1. If you like Rip Van Winkle had fallen asleep for the past decade, you'd be surprised by the changes in today's electronic culture.

2. You'd suddenly discover the Digital Age a time of rapid development in electronic technology had come while you were sleeping.

3. You'd realize that your old television a bulky thing with an often fuzzy picture was now flat against the wall with crystal-clear images.

4. If you went to purchase a flat screen television, you could choose between plasma display a gel medium or LCD a liquid crystal display for your living room screen.

5. You could choose when to watch any program, or watch several shows at once "picture in picture" on the same screen, and this might even be built into your refrigerator to enjoy while you cooked supper.

6. You would probably not even have to walk across the room to answer the phone, because it would be a compact portable, or you'd be wearing a miniature device a lightweight headset allowing you to listen and talk hands-free.

7. You could keep up with your job from almost anywhere working on your wireless laptop a small, lightweight portable computer with worldwide web access.

8. Always on the go, you could get your mail electronically, send typed text messages, chat with several people at once or play a game, or even take

photos or video clips, all from the palm of your hand on a cellular phone now a multifunctional device with built-in computer.

9. Thanks to compact DVD players digital video disk devices you could watch your favourite film from the back seat of your car while travelling with friends.

10. At the mall, you'd notice many young people ten year olds to teens moving to a tune in their heads.

11. This tune in their heads would be coming through a tiny device an MP3 with tiny earphones as they listened to their choice of hundreds of songs downloaded from their computer to the media player.

12. Miniaturization and digitization would have made much of this possible, and communications satellites constantly orbiting would be bouncing signals around the earth for everything from the nightly newscast to your phone call to Hong Kong.

13. The electronic age just science fiction before really is "out of this world."

14. But perhaps it's not all good; when your "office" a small portable device in your hand is always with you, how do you escape from work?

15. You might ask whether the convenience of full-time access to information and people outweighs the necessity of having to deal with it all.

16. And parents and teachers remembering pre-electronic times ask whether young people once good readers now need to be constantly entertained.

17. But good or bad, personal electronic devices compact and inexpensive are here to stay.

Exercise 14B

▶ Add commas and semicolons to the following essay wherever they are needed. This exercise covers the punctuation of both appositives and parenthetical expressions.

Many Canadians people who have immigrated from all over the world are unaware of the contributions of those with African, African-American or Caribbean ancestry to this country's development. Often they are unaware that Canada just north of the United States even allowed slavery.

It wasn't until the Abolition Act of 1793 made Ontario then called Upper Canada the first British-controlled territory to outlaw slavery, although alas it would be forty years before the Act became official.

How many of us know that Mathieu Da Costa an interpreter for Samuel de Champlain was the first recorded person of African descent in Canada in the early 1600s? Or that Josiah Henson the inspiration for Harriet Beecher Stowe's anti-slavery novel *Uncle Tom's Cabin* escaped to live in Canada? Nonetheless the name Harriet Tubman is well known. She helped over three hundred American slaves come to freedom in Canada through the Underground Railway a loose network of safe houses.

It was a free black woman born in the United States Mary Ann Shadd who became Canada's first female newspaper editor and first female black lawyer. She had come to Windsor Ontario in 1851 there she was a teacher and activist for integration. As a matter of fact she set up the first school a private one open to children of all colours.

Of course many of us know the saying "The Real McCoy" meaning the genuine thing. But do we know that it refers to a Canadian of African heritage Elijah McCoy an engineer who because of his colour toiled as a railroad worker? He invented an oil lubricating cup that saved steam engines from overheating.

Blacks in Canada although from diverse backgrounds and cultures have one thing in common they have endured racism. Many have faced discrimination to fight for the British and later the Canadian armed services. In 1857 naval officer William Edward Hall the son of a freed slave was the first Canadian and the first person of African roots to receive the Victoria Cross the British Empire's highest military honour for his role in India. Black Loyalists those loyal to Britain after the American Revolution aided Canadians in the War of 1812. Because of discrimination, an all-black battalion was formed to serve in the First World War furthermore it wasn't until near the end of the Second World War that black volunteers were fully accepted. Many served with great distinction.

It was Jean Augustine Canada's first black woman elected to Parliament who helped establish Black History Month across Canada. Toronto home to people of all colours had been celebrating the achievements of Blacks in February since 1979. A 1995 decree made it official across the nation. Now all Canadians can acknowledge the contributions of Black Canadians. And in 2006 the installation of the Right Honourable Michaëlle Jean as Governor General became an inspiration to all especially women and those sharing her Afro-Caribbean heritage.

Whether journalists, athletes, business entrepreneurs, politicians, doctors, artists, entertainers or educators, newcomers or sixth-generation Canadians, black men and women those with African or Caribbean heritage have contributed much to our national fabric.

Restrictive and
Nonrestrictive Clauses

In Chapter 14 you learned that if a phrase adds extra information about a noun that has already been specifically identified, that phrase (an **appositive**) must be set off by commas. For example,

Many of CBC's television shows are filmed in Vancouver, *a Pacific Coast city known for its scenery and mild climate.*

The appositive is set off by commas because the place in which many of CBC's television shows are filmed has already been specifically identified as *Vancouver*.

On the other hand, if a phrase is necessary to establish the specific identity of a noun, the phrase is *not* set off by commas.

The verb *to be* is the most irregular verb in the English language.

The phrase *to be* is not set off by commas because it is necessary to identify which specific verb is the most irregular verb in the English language.

The same rule that applies to the punctuation of appositive phrases also applies to the punctuation of *clauses*. Read the following sentences, in which the dependent clauses have been italicized. Can you see why one sentence in each pair has commas while the other does not?

The woman *whom you have just met* is in charge of the program.

Teresa Gomez, *whom you have just met,* is in charge of the program.

The book *that I am now reading* is an anthology of short stories and poetry by Canadian writers of African descent.

Fiery Spirits, which I am now reading, is an anthology of short stories and poetry by Canadian writers of African descent.

In the first sentence of each pair, the dependent clause is necessary to establish the specific identity of the noun it follows. This type of clause is called a **restrictive** clause because it *restricts,* or limits, the meaning of the word it describes. For example, in the first sentence if the restrictive clause were removed, the sentence would read:

The woman is in charge of the program.

The meaning of this sentence is unclear because there are billions of women in the world, and any one of them might be in charge of the program. But when the clause is added to the sentence, the meaning of the general word *woman* is now restricted, or limited, to *one particular woman—the woman whom you have just met*. Thus, the restrictive clause "whom you have just met" establishes the specific identity of the word *woman*.

Similarly, in the third sentence above, the clause "that I am now reading" identifies *which* book is an anthology of writing by Canadian writers of African descent. It restricts the general word *book* to *one particular book—the book that I am now reading*.

Because restrictive clauses are necessary to establish the specific identity of the nouns they describe, the following punctuation rule applies:

Restrictive clauses are not set off by commas.

In contrast, the clauses in the second and fourth sentences are *not* necessary to identify which particular woman is in charge of the program or which particular book is an anthology of writing by Canadian writers of African descent. In these sentences, the woman has already been identified as *Teresa Gomez,* and the book has already been identified as *Fiery Spirits*. Because these clauses are *not* restrictive clauses, they are called **nonrestrictive clauses**. Nonrestrictive clauses merely add extra information about the nouns they describe. They serve the same function as appositives and are punctuated in the same way.

Nonrestrictive clauses must be completely set off from the rest of the sentence by commas.

This means that if a nonrestrictive clause is at the *end* of a sentence, it will be *preceded* by a comma. If it is in the *middle* of a sentence, it will be *both preceded and followed* by a comma. (Like appositives, nonrestrictive clauses never occur at the beginning of a sentence because they must follow the noun that they describe.)

The restrictive and nonrestrictive clauses that you have been studying are called adjective clauses because, like adjectives, these clauses describe nouns. The words that most frequently introduce adjective clauses are:

that

where

which

who

whom

whose

Like all clauses, adjective clauses must contain both a subject and a verb. But notice that in adjective clauses *the word that introduces the clause may also be the subject of the clause.*

S   V

The house *that once occupied this lot* was destroyed by fire.

Or the clause may contain a separate subject:

S V

The wallet *that I lost* contained all my credit cards.

Adjective clauses, like adverb clauses, are used in **complex sentences.** Although these sentences may not seem to be complex at first glance, if you study the sentences above, you will see that each of them has two subjects and two verbs. Also, if the adjective clause, which is the **dependent clause,** is removed from the sentence, a complete independent clause remains.

S   V

INDEPENDENT CLAUSE   The house was destroyed by fire.

	S V
DEPENDENT CLAUSE	that once occupied this lot

	S V
INDEPENDENT CLAUSE	The wallet contained all my credit cards.

	S V
DEPENDENT CLAUSE	that I lost

An adjective clause often occurs in the middle of a sentence because it must follow the noun it describes. When an adjective clause is in the middle of a sentence, part of the independent clause precedes it, and the rest of the independent clause follows it. For example,

        S   V

Food *that is high in calories* often tastes better than low-calorie food.

                     S   V

The National Museum of Civilization, *which is Canada's most popular cultural institution,* is across from the Parliament Buildings.

A sentence may contain more than one adjective clause. Each clause is punctuated separately. In the following sentences, the first adjective clause is *nonrestrictive* (with commas), and the second clause is *restrictive* (no commas).

The ice storm, *which caused prolonged power outages,* taught people survival skills *that are essential in winter.*

Algonquin Park, *which covers 7,725 square kilometres of forests, lakes, and rivers,* was named after the early First Nations people *who inhabited the area.*

▶   Underline every adjective clause in each of the following sentences, and circle the noun it describes. Then decide which clauses are restrictive (and do *not* need commas) and which clauses are nonrestrictive (and *do* need commas). Add the appropriate punctuation.

Note: Although clauses beginning with *who, whom, whose,* or *where* may be either restrictive or nonrestrictive, clauses that begin with *that* are *always* restrictive. In addition, many writers prefer to use *which* only for nonrestrictive clauses.

The intersection of Portage and Main which is in downtown Winnipeg is known for its cold winds in winter.

The classes that I am taking this semester are all easy for me.

Most tourists who come to Whitehorse in the Yukon also visit Dawson City which is over 500 kilometres north of the city.

The candidate whom we supported was not elected.

Ms. Gomez whose native language is Spanish also speaks French, German, and English.

She is an artist whom we all admire a great deal.

EXERCISE 15A

▶ Each of the following sentences contains one or more adjective clauses. Underline each adjective clause, and circle the noun or pronouns it describes. If the clause is nonrestrictive and needs additional punctuation, add a comma or commas wherever necessary. If all of the adjective clauses in a sentence are restrictive and the sentence needs no additional punctuation, label it C for *correct*.

1. The first American television commercial which was an image of a Bulova watch face was broadcast in New York on July 1, 1941.

2. The image was projected on a screen at Ebbets Field where the Dodgers and Phillies were playing a baseball game.

3. The fee that Bulova paid to broadcast this commercial which was a remarkably low nine dollars seems unbelievable by today's standards.

4. Now, of course, advertisers spend millions of dollars to place commercials on programs that attract large numbers of viewers.

5. Social critics are now studying the effects that television commercials may have on our lives.

6. A slogan that appears in an especially memorable commercial may later be used in ways that have nothing to do with the original product.

7. For example, the 1960s ad slogan "Mother, please, I'd rather do it myself!" which appeared in commercials for the pain-killer Anacin was adopted by a generation of teenagers as a declaration of resistance to parental control.

8. Millions of teenagers saw the Anacin commercial during the Beatles' appearance on the Ed Sullivan Show which was one of the most popular variety shows of that era.

9. Another famous slogan that also achieved national fame appeared in a series of commercials for Wendy's hamburgers.

10. The Wendy's slogan which was "Where's the beef?" became a popular way of describing political proposals that promised more than they could reasonably hope to deliver.

11. Of course, the real purpose of commercials is to encourage viewers to buy the products that are being advertised.

12. Advertisers are now exploring new venues that include commercials made just for viewing on the Internet.

13. Every e-mail user is also familiar with the unwanted commercial messages that are known as "spam."

14. Internet spam should not be confused with SPAM which is the name of a commercial meat product made by the Hormel Company.

15. The TiVo which enables viewers to delete commercials and other similar recording devices may pose a danger to advertisers using the older medium of television.

16. However, as long as there are consumers who are willing to buy products, it is difficult to imagine a world without commercials of some sort.

EXERCISE 15B

▶ Add commas and semicolons to the following sentences wherever they are necessary. This exercise covers the punctuation of parenthetical expressions, appositives, and restrictive and nonrestrictive clauses. If a sentence needs no additional punctuation, mark it C for *correct*.

1. *Eponyms* are words that are derived from people's names.

2. The eponym that is probably the most familiar is the word *sandwich*.

3. The sandwich was named for an 18th-century English nobleman John Montague whose official title was the fourth Earl of Sandwich.

4. The earl was a gambler who often played cards for hours at a time.

5. He disliked having to interrupt his gaming to eat meals therefore he asked his cook to prepare a snack that he could eat at the gaming table.

6. Montague also wanted a snack that he could eat with one hand so that he would have one hand left to hold his cards.

7. The cook complied by preparing the first sandwich which consisted of two slices of beef between two pieces of toast.

8. Another eponym is the word *boycott* which also has an interesting history.

9. During the 19th century, most of the farmland in Ireland was owned by absentee landlords who were English and who charged their Irish tenant farmers high rents.

10. Charles Boycott who was the local agent for one of the English landlords refused to meet his tenants' demands for lower rent.

11. As a result Boycott's Irish neighbours decided to punish him by acting as if he were a person who no longer existed.

12. No one would speak to him, work for him, or sell him the products that he needed to operate his estate.

13. Today, people still use Boycott's name when they refuse to deal with people or businesses that have treated them unfairly.

14. A famous example in American history is the 1955–56 Montgomery, Alabama bus boycott which began after Rosa Parks was arrested for sitting in the white section of a Montgomery city bus.

15. Another eponym is the word *silhouette* which is a black ink portrait that shows only the outline in profile of a person's face.

16. Silhouettes are drawings that can be finished in only a few minutes thus they were a cheap alternative to the expensive and time-consuming process of having a portrait painted in oils.

17. Because silhouettes show only a minimum amount of detail, their name was meant to poke fun at a French minister of finance Etienne de Silhouette who constantly attempted to reduce expenditures to a bare minimum.

18. Other commonly used eponyms include the months of July and August which were named after two Roman emperors Julius and Augustus Caesar.

19. Levis which are a common name for a brand of blue jeans are named after Levi Strauss who made heavy work pants for miners during the California gold rush.

20. Another article of clothing that is named after a person is the leotard a one-piece garment often worn by dancers and gymnasts.

21. It was designed by Jules Leotard a famous 19th-century French trapeze artist.

22. Leotard wanted to wear a close-fitting garment that called attention to his athletic physique.

23. Eponyms are words that remind us of people and events in the past; they are therefore a kind of souvenir of the history of our language.

Items in a Series and Dates and Addresses

A *series* consists of *three* or *more* related items. Commas are placed between each item in a series.

> *Danish, Swedish,* and *Norwegian* are related languages.

> For dessert you may choose *ice cream, sherbet,* or *tapioca.*

> To qualify for this job, you must have *a master's degree in international relations, at least three years of work experience,* and *the ability to speak both Spanish and Portuguese.*

Although some writers consider the final comma before the conjunction (*and, or,* or *nor*) optional, using it is preferred, especially in formal writing.

However, if *every* item in a series is joined by a conjunction, no commas are needed because the conjunctions keep the individual items separated. This type of construction is used only when the writer wishes to place particular emphasis on the number of items in the series.

The backyard of this house has a *swimming pool* and *a Jacuzzi* and *a hot tub*.

If a **date** or an **address** consists of more than one item, a comma is used after *each* part of the date or the address, *including a comma after the last item.* (If the last item in the series is also the last word in the sentence, only a period follows it.) Notice that this punctuation rule differs from the rule used for punctuating an ordinary series.

My grandparents will celebrate their fiftieth wedding anniversary on October 11, 2008, with a party for all of their family.

The name of the month and the number of the day (October 11) are considered a single item and are separated from the year by a comma. However, notice that a comma also *follows* 2008, which is the last item in the date.

We moved from Kenora, Ontario, to Trois-Rivières, Quebec, in 1995.

Notice the commas after "Ontario" and "Quebec." These commas are used in addition to the commas that separate the names of the cities from the names of the provinces.

If a date or an address consists of only a single item, no comma is necessary.

December 25 is Christmas.
We moved from Ontario to Quebec.

A comma is not used before a postal code number.

His mailing address in Unionville is Markham, Ontario L3R 6J2.

▶   Punctuate the following sentences.

The armistice signed on November 11, 1918 ended the fighting in the First World War.

Because of the multicultural character of my neighbourhood, church bazaars sell tacos pizza teriyaki chow mein and hot dogs.

The coffee shop's special club sandwich contains ham and cheese and turkey.

I can't believe that you drove from Kingston Ontario to Regina Saskatchewan in three days.

John F. Kennedy Aldous Huxley and C. S. Lewis all died on November 22 1963.

EXERCISE 16A

▶ Add commas to the following sentences wherever they are needed. If a sentence needs no additional commas, label it C for *correct*. This exercise covers only the punctuation rules from Chapter 16.

1. When the first Harry Potter book, *Harry Potter and the Philosopher's Stone,* was published in London England in September 1998 few people anticipated how incredibly successful the entire series would be.

2. The very next year, J. K. Rowling published two more volumes, *Harry Potter and the Chamber of Secrets* on June 2 1999 and *Harry Potter and the Prisoner of Azkaban* on September 8th.

3. On June 8 2000 the fourth volume in the series, *Harry Potter and the Goblet of Fire,* appeared, but it took Rowling three years to finish *Harry Potter and the Order of the Phoenix,* which was published on June 21 2003.

4. However, Rowling is not England's only fantasy writer, for in April 1995 Philip Pullman published the first book in his fantasy series, *His Dark Materials.*

5. The three volumes that make up this series are *The Golden Compass The Subtle Knife* and *The Amber Spyglass.*

6. The British National Theatre presented a stage version of the entire series that ran from November 20 2004 to April 2 2005.

7. Theatre critics and audiences loved the production because of its special effects wonderful acting and entertaining plot.

8. The works of Rowling and Pullman are examples of a genre known as high fantasy; its characteristics include a setting in an imaginary world a hero on a quest and a battle between the forces of good and evil.

9. The Carter family is planning an end-of-the-year vacation that will take them from their home in Sudbury Ontario to San Francisco California.

10. They will stay in San Francisco from December 26 2007 through January 4 2008.

11. In order to plan their trip, they contacted the San Francisco Convention and Visitors Bureau at 201 Third Street Suite 900 San Francisco California 94103.

12. The Bureau sent them maps of the city a list of places to visit and even discount coupons for restaurants and shops.

13. If the Carters need more information, they could also contact the San Francisco Visitor Information Center, which has personnel on site and telephone operators who speak English Spanish French Italian and Japanese.

14. Because accommodations in the suburbs are less expensive than those in the city, the Carters will stay at the Days Inn, whose address is 3255 Geneva Avenue Daly City California 94014.

15. The family loves to try new restaurants, and they are looking forward to dining in a city that is equally famous for its French and Chinese and Italian cuisine.

EXERCISE 16B

▶ Add commas and semicolons to the following wherever they are necessary. This exercise covers the punctuation of items in a series, dates and addresses, restrictive and nonrestrictive clauses, appositives, and parenthetical expressions.

Winter unfortunately can mean many long and dark months for those living in northern regions. How do people who live in such a climate overcome the depression and inactivity of winter?

Many Canadian communities small or large hold winter festivals or carnivals. Naturally participating in a festival gets people outdoors who might otherwise stay inside. From St. John's Newfoundland to Inuvik Northwest Territories friends and neighbours and town officials and visitors all come together to chase away the winter doldrums.

Winter celebrations include activities as diverse as curling bonspiels hockey tournaments snowmobile treks children's games on frozen ponds horse-drawn sleigh rides and smooshing races.

What you may ask is "smooshing?" This sport has two people sharing a pair of ski-like boards with foot straps for each it requires coordination and cooperation to say the least.

Many festivals feature pancake eating or in the case of Moosejaw Saskatchewan pancake tossing contests. Often there are costume parades haywagon or dogsled rides and open-air concerts. Niagara Falls Ontario boasts a festival of lights the Okanagan Valley British Columbia hosts an ice wine festival each January. However perhaps the best-known carnival is Carnaval in Quebec City Quebec.

Billed as "The World's Biggest Winter Carnival" Carnaval is held for two weeks at the end of January. Originally a chance to party before the self-denial of the Christian Lenten season the first large carnival took place in January 1894. Bonhomme representing all that Carnaval symbolizes was put in place in 1954. A giant snowman character he wears the folkloric red waist scarf and toque a winter cap.

Carnaval centres on street parties with music food and even the powerful alcoholic "Caribou" drink believed to have been invented on Ste-Thérèse Street lower Quebec City. There is a giant Ice Palace surrounded by snow sculptures. The snow sculpture contest which began in January 1973 has grown to represent artists from over thirty countries showcasing their talents.

Quebec's city streets covered in snow become a trail for the dogsled races which start from the Château Frontenac and continue along Saint-Louis Street Grand Allée and the Plains of Abraham to end back at the imposing hotel.

Begun in the late 19th century the Château Frontenac was built by William Van Horne General Manager of the Canadian Pacific Railway. It was named after Louis de Buade Count of Frontenac governor of New France from 1672 to 1698. Visitors can contact the hotel at 1 rue des Carrieres Quebec City Quebec Canada G1R 4P5.

For sure Canadians know how to make the most of winter a time of long cold days and keep community spirits high by holding winter celebrations.

Unit 4 Review

▶ Add commas and semicolons to the following essay wherever they are necessary. This exercise covers the punctuation of parenthetical expressions, direct address, appositives, restrictive and nonrestrictive clauses, series, and dates and addresses.

Many comic strips have devoted readers however few strips have achieved the popularity of *Peanuts*. Original strips appeared for nearly fifty years, from October 2 1950 to February 13 2000 ending only with the death of their creator Charles Schulz. Moreover re-runs of the strip still appear in newspapers throughout the world.

Charles Schulz was born on November 26 1922 in St. Paul Minnesota. His own childhood experiences provided part of the content for the *Peanuts* strip. He skipped two grades in elementary school therefore he was the youngest student in his freshman high school class and, like Charlie Brown, often felt shy and isolated. There are other parallels between Schulz's life and that of Charlie Brown. For example both had fathers who were barbers both owned dogs and both were in love with a red-haired girl. The real-life redhead was Donna Johnston who was an accountant at the art school where Schulz taught classes. Johnston refused Schulz's marriage proposal nevertheless they remained friends for the rest of his life.

Schulz actually hated the name *Peanuts* which was given to the strip by its publishers. Schulz's original name for the strip *Good Ol' Charlie Brown* was meant to honour its central character. Another main character was Snoopy Charlie Brown's pet beagle. There were also crabby Lucy van Pelt and Linus who was Lucy's younger brother. Linus of course became famous for his devotion to his blanket and his belief in the myth of the Halloween Great Pumpkin.

Although the strip ran for nearly fifty years, in general the characters were children who did not age. They remained forever in the third grade. An exception was Linus who was introduced to the strip as an infant. However he gradually became the same age as Charlie Brown. Additional characters were introduced to the strip during the 1960s. One of the most prominent was Peppermint Patty who consistently received "D" grades on school assignments. As a result Patty often had to attend summer school instead of joining the other characters at summer camp. However Schulz also used his strip to poke fun at teachers. In one strip for example Linus was asked to write a composition about what he did during the summer which is the standard writing assignment for the first day of the fall semester. Linus raised his hand and asked, "Miss Othmar how do you teachers keep coming up with such original topics?" The last major addition to the strip was Rerun van Pelt who is Lucy and Linus's younger brother.

In 1965, the *Peanuts* characters appeared in their first television special which was titled *A Charlie Brown Christmas*. The success of this show led to other holiday specials for instance *It's the Great Pumpkin, Charlie Brown*. Eventually, more than thirty television specials were produced. Because the television programs were so well received, the first *Peanuts* feature film *A Boy Named Charlie Brown* appeared in 1968. It was followed by three other feature films, none of which by the way contained the word *Peanuts* in their titles.

The legacy of Charles Schulz and of the *Peanuts* characters is preserved in the Charles M. Schulz Museum which opened on August 17 2002 and is located at 2301 Hardies Lane Santa Rosa California 95403. The museum includes a replica of Schulz's studio an outdoor Snoopy labyrinth and a vast collection of original *Peanuts* comic strips. Even small details from the strips are there. For example Charlie Brown was never able to fly his kite successfully. Unfortunately it always ended up being caught in a tree. Therefore if you look up at one of the trees in the museum courtyard, you will see a kite that is firmly stuck among the tree's branches. It is a fitting tribute to the hapless Charlie Brown and his many misadventures.

Unit 5

Pronoun Usage

Subject, Object,
and Possessive Pronouns

Pronouns are words that are used to refer to persons, places, things, and ideas without repeating their names. In other words, pronouns are used in place of nouns. For example, rather than saying "Ben lost Ben's notebook last night, but Ben found the notebook this morning," you can say, "Ben lost *his* notebook last night, but *he* found *it* this morning." In this sentence, the pronoun *his* replaces Ben's, the pronoun *he* replaces Ben, and the pronoun *it* replaces notebook. The noun that the pronoun replaces is called the **antecedent** (Latin for "to go before") of the pronoun.

There are several different kinds of pronouns, but in this lesson you will be studying only **subject pronouns, object pronouns,** and **possessive pronouns.**

Singular Pronouns

Subject	Object	Possessive	Possessive Adjectives
I	me	mine	my
you	you	yours	your
he	him	his	his
she	her	hers	her
it	it	its	its

Plural Pronouns

Subject	Object	Possessive	Possessive Adjectives
we	us	ours	our
you	you	yours	your
they	them	theirs	their

As their name suggests, **subject pronouns** are used as the subject of a sentence or a clause. For example,

He is a good dancer.

We went to the park together.

In *formal* speech and writing, subject pronouns are also used after forms of the verb *be,* as in:

That is *she* singing with the chorus.

It is *I* who need your help.

If I were *she,* I'd have come to the lecture.

In formal speech and writing, subject pronouns are used after forms of the verb *be* because they refer to the *same* thing or person as the subject.

That = she singing with the chorus.

It = I.

I = she.

However, in *informal* speech, many people would use object pronouns in the sentences below.

That is (or That's) *her* singing with the chorus.

It is (or It's) *me*.

If I were *her*, I'd have come to the lecture.

Whether you choose to say "it is I" or "it is me" depends on the circumstances. If you are taking an English test or writing a formal essay, using subject pronouns after forms of *be* is appropriate and expected. But if you are speaking casually with a friend, "It is I" may sound artificial, and the informal "It is me" might be more suitable.

In this unit, you will be studying both grammar and usage. Try to keep clear in your mind those situations in which you have a choice between formal and informal constructions (usage) and those situations in which only one pronoun form is correct at all times (grammar).

"It is *we*" versus "It is *us*" = usage.

"Ali and *I* are here" versus "Ali and *me* are here" = grammar.

Object pronouns are used as objects of prepositions, as direct objects, and as indirect objects.

You will remember that the noun or pronoun in a prepositional phrase is called **the object of the preposition.** That is why an object pronoun replaces the noun. For example,

The award was given to *Alexei*.

The award was given to *him*.

Please sit by *Katy*.

Please sit by *her*.

Object pronouns are also used as direct objects. A **direct object** is the word that *receives* the action of the verb and, with very few exceptions, follows the verb, often as the next word.

      S   DO
The artist painted that *picture*.

The artist painted *it*.

   S   DO
He composed that *song* last night.

He composed *it* last night.

Another way that object pronouns are used is as indirect objects. An **indirect object** is the person or thing *to whom* or *for whom* something is done.

S   IO   DO

She made *Robert* a chocolate cake.

She made *him* a chocolate cake.

The preceding sentence is another way of saying, "She made a chocolate cake *for him.*"

S   IO DO

Benjamin gave his *sister* a gift.

Benjamin gave *her* a gift.

The preceding sentence is another way of saying, "Benjamin gave a gift to *her.*"
Possessive pronouns and adjectives are used to show ownership.

The cat scratched *its* neck. (adjective)

The children stamped *their* feet in joy. (adjective)

Very few people make pronoun errors when there is only one subject or one object in a sentence. For example, no native speaker of English would say, "Us is here" instead of "We are here." *However, people often do make mistakes when two subjects or two objects are paired up in a sentence.* For example, which of the following two sentences is grammatically correct?

Chantal bought Kevin and *me* some good cookies.

Chantal bought Kevin and *I* some good cookies.

To determine the correct pronoun in this kind of "double" construction, split the sentence in two like this:

1. Chantal bought Kevin some good cookies.
2. Chantal bought (me, I) some good cookies.

As you can tell after you have split the sentence in two, it would be incorrect to say, "Chantal bought *I* some good cookies." The correct pronoun is *me*, which is the indirect object of the verb *bought*. Therefore, the whole sentence should read:

Chantal bought Kevin and me some good cookies.

▶ Which of the following two sentences is correct?

The mayor congratulated Carlos and *I.*

The mayor congratulated Carlos and *me.*

Again, split the sentences in two.

1. The mayor congratulated Carlos.
2. The mayor congratulated (me, I).

Now, which pronoun is correct?

Another very common pronoun error is using subject pronouns instead of object pronouns after prepositions. The object of a preposition must be an
▶ *object pronoun.* Which of the following two sentences is correct?

The teacher handed new books to Sam and *I.*

The teacher handed new books to Sam and *me.*

If you split the sentence in two, you have:

1. The teacher handed new books to Sam.
2. The teacher handed new books to (me, I).

The correct pronoun is *me,* which is the object of the preposition *to.* Therefore, the correct sentence is:

The teacher handed new books to Sam and *me.*

It is extremely important that you do not decide which pronoun to use simply on the basis of what "sounds better" *unless you split the sentence in two first.* To many people, "The teacher handed new books to Sam and I" sounds "more correct" than "The teacher handed new books to Sam and *me,*" yet, as you have seen, *me* is actually the correct pronoun.

Another example of choosing an incorrect pronoun because it "sounds better" is the frequent misuse of the subject pronoun *I* after the preposition *between.* As you already know, the object of a preposition must be an *object* pronoun. Therefore, it is always incorrect to say "between you and *I.*" The correct construction is "between you and *me.*"

▶   Circle the pronoun that correctly completes each of the following sentences.

Between you and (I, me), that's a wonderful movie.

The teacher rewarded Joseph and (I, me) for our presentation.

Ken and (she, her) speak frequently.

Helene made Sasha and (I, me) Halloween costumes.

The party was for their class and (we, us).

Occasionally you may use constructions like the following:

We freshmen must pre-enroll for our classes.

Most of *us nurses* would prefer to work the 7 A.M. to 3 P.M. shift.

To determine whether the sentence requires a subject or an object pronoun, see which pronoun would be correct if the pronoun appeared in the sentence by itself rather than being followed by a noun.

(We, us) citizens should vote in each election.

(We, us) should vote in each election.

Give a raise to (we, us) good workers.

Give a raise to (we, us).

The correct pronouns are *we* citizens and *us* workers.

▶   Circle the pronoun that correctly completes each of the following sentences.

Some theatres give a discount to (we, us) students.

Actors depend on the support of (we, us) fans.

(We, us) customers want the store to stay open later.

EXERCISE 17A

▶ The first part of this exercise is intended for a quick review of subject and object pronouns. Reverse each sentence so that the subject pronoun becomes the object and the object pronoun becomes the subject.

> Example: *They* offered *me* some cookies.
> Answer: *I* offered *them* some cookies.

1. *They* brought the papers to *me*.

2. *She* opened the door for *him*.

3. *You* gave *us* great advice.

4. *He* rode the subway with *me* for several years.

5. *I* explained the project to *them*.

6. *We* invited *him* to the party.

▶ Circle the pronoun that correctly completes each sentence. Remember to split the sentence first if it contains a "double" construction. Apply the rules of formal English usage.

7. The class collected flowers for Lucas and (I, me).

8. (We, Us) citizens should never forget how important it is to exercise our right to vote in each election.

9. It was (he, him) who sent you that card.

10. If I were (she, her), I'd keep away from anyone who lies.

11. The coach's message to (we, us) players is to go out and win the game!

12. Between you and (I, me), I think his performance wasn't very good.

13. Send Jodi and (he, him) the final draft of your new song.

14. Once a month, three of my closest friends and (I, me) meet for lunch.

15. When (we, us) neighbours get together, everyone has a wonderful time.

16. (She, Her) and her boyfriend enjoy seeing action movies.

17. Nisanthini thanked André and (I, me) for her birthday gift.

18. Sarah and (he, him) have a lot of trouble getting to work on time.

19. Most of (we, us) students wanted the class to start a little later.

20. The surprise party made Sean and (we, us) very happy.

EXERCISE 17B

▶ Some of the following sentences contain pronoun errors. Cross out the incorrect pronouns, and write in the correct forms. If a sentence contains no pronoun errors, label it C for *correct*. Apply the rules of formal English usage.

1. Our neighbours invited my husband and I to their barbeque.

2. An increase in tuition is a hardship for we students.

3. Alice and he often carpool to work together.

4. If I were them, I wouldn't try to sell a house during the Christmas holidays.

5. The argument is between Marja and her boss, not between Marja and I.

6. It is us, not our competitors, who can give your company the best service.

7. My friends and me often play basketball on the weekends.

8. Eva never knew it was him who was spreading false rumours about her.

9. Us citizens need to vote in the next election.

10. She and I have known each other since elementary school.

11. The high school dance is being chaperoned by Ellie, her husband, and I.

12. The company's decision to move production overseas will cost we employees hundreds of jobs.

13. Leave the key with Ram or us when you leave.

14. The time has come for they and us to settle our dispute.

15. Don't complain to the other employees and I about your personal problems.

16. Just between you and I, don't you think our town needs a new mayor?

17. If it were up to Hailey and I, all of the workers would have a longer lunch hour.

18. If I were him, I wouldn't change jobs now.

19. Give copies of your report to he and his partners.

20. With Jiang and she helping us, we can finish this project on time.

Pronouns in Comparisons and Pronouns with *-self, -selves*

USING PRONOUNS IN COMPARISONS

In speech and in writing, we often compare two people or two things with each other. For example,

> *Rosa* is older than *I* am.

> The company pays *Nazeem* a higher salary than it pays *me*.

In the sentences above, it is easy to tell whether a subject pronoun or an object pronoun should be used in each comparison. In the first sentence, the subject pronoun *I* is correct because it would be clearly ungrammatical to say "Rosa is older than *me* am." In the second sentence, the object pronoun *me* is correct because you would not say "The company pays Nazeem a higher salary than it pays *I*."

When writing, however, people usually do not express comparisons in full, but use a shortened form instead. For example,

Iole plays tennis better than *I*.

The accident injured Sami more than *me*.

In these cases, it is possible to determine which pronoun is correct by mentally filling in the words that have been left out of the comparison.

Iole plays tennis better than I (do).

The accident injured Sami more than (it injured) me.

▶   Fill in the missing words to determine which pronouns are correct in the following sentences:

Clarence can run longer distances than (I, me).

I enjoy classical music more than (he, him).

This trip will be more interesting for you than (she, her).

That dress looks better on you than (she, her).

Doing sit-ups is easier for you than (I, me).

When you fill in the missing words, the correct comparisons are

Clarence can run longer distances than *I* (can).

I enjoy classical music more than *he* (does).

This trip will be more interesting for you than (it will be for) *her*.

That dress looks better on you than (it does on) *her*.

Doing sit-ups is easier for you than (it is for) *me*.

In *informal* usage, you often hear people use object pronouns instead of subject pronouns in comparisons (for example, "He's taller than me" instead of "He's taller than I"). However, these forms are generally considered inappropriate in writing and formal speech. You should be especially careful in situations where the wrong pronoun can change the meaning of the entire sentence. For example, "Charlotte danced with Ryan more than *I* (danced with him)" does not mean the same thing as "Charlotte danced with Ryan more than (she danced with) *me*." In addition, using the wrong pronoun can sometimes lead to unintentionally ridiculous sentences, such as the following:

My husband likes sports more than me.

Unless the husband happens to like sports more than he likes his wife, the correct pronoun would be:

My husband likes sports more than *I* (do).

(Note: The conjunction *than,* which is used in comparisons, should not be confused with the adverb *then,* which indicates next in time.)

AVOIDING DOUBLED SUBJECTS

Do not "double," or repeat, the subject of a sentence by repeating the noun in its pronoun form.

INCORRECT	My sister, she is a nurse.
CORRECT	My sister is a nurse.
INCORRECT	The Smalls, they are our neighbours.
CORRECT	The Smalls are our neighbours.

PRONOUNS WITH -SELF, -SELVES

Some pronouns end in *-self* or *-selves*:

Singular	*Plural*
myself	ourselves
yourself	yourselves
himself	themselves
herself	
itself	

These pronouns can be used in two ways. They can be **reflexive pronouns.** Reflexive pronouns are used when the object of the verb or the object of the preposition is the same person or thing as the subject. For example,

I cut *myself.* (myself = I)

They will do the job by *themselves.* (themselves = they)

Suzanne enjoyed *herself* at the party. (herself = Suzanne)

Or they may be used for **emphasis.**

Frank *himself* admits that he is lazy.

Her husband is a famous composer, and she *herself* is a well-known singer.

We *ourselves* are responsible for our decisions.

Notice that the singular forms of reflexive pronouns end in *-self,* and the plural forms end in *-selves.* In standard English, there are no such forms as *hisself, ourselfs, theirselfs,* or *themselfs.* These forms are considered nonstandard in both speech and writing and should be avoided unless you are using a dialect, such as you might do in writing a story.

In formal English, the reflexive pronoun *myself* is NOT used in place of a subject or an object pronoun.

INCORRECT	Luis and myself are going out.
CORRECT	Luis and I are going out.
INCORRECT	The director asked Karol and myself to read the script.
CORRECT	The director asked Karol and me to read the script.

Myself is sometimes used as a subject or an object pronoun in informal usage, but even in these cases the use of the correct subject or object pronoun is preferred. Referring to yourself as *myself,* rather than as *I* or *me,* does *not* make you sound more polite or more modest.

EXERCISE 18A

▶ **Part 1:** Circle the pronoun that most logically and correctly completes each sentence. Apply the rules of formal English usage. This exercise covers *only* the rules in Chapter 18.

1. Jessica is a far better writer than (I, me).

2. A change in routine upsets her children more than (she, her).

3. Philip and (I, me, myself) climbed onto the roof to rescue the cat.

4. The law students congratulated (theirselves, themselves) for passing the bar exam.

5. No one knows better than (they, them) how hard that exam was.

6. Our friend gave Paolo and (I, me, myself) tickets to the opera.

▶ **Part 2:** Correct any pronoun errors that appear in the following sentences. If a sentence has no pronoun errors, label it C for *correct*. These sentences cover rules from Chapters 17 and 18.

7. My father taught my brother and myself how to manage our finances.

8. He and me are happier than her.

9. The children want to walk the dog all by theirselves.

10. Between you and I, this party is boring, so let's leave now.

11. Us pet lovers need to organize an animal rescue group.

12. She loves her new car better than me.

13. The presents for you and him are in the hall closet.

14. Did you let the children walk to school all by themselfs?

15. My boyfriend he plans to go skiing this weekend.

16. Her and her boyfriend like to study together.

17. The new action movie has just enough excitement for my friends and me.

18. The puppy brings you and I so much happiness.

19. Did you build that doghouse yourself?

20. I work much longer hours than him.

EXERCISE 18B

▶ Cross out any pronoun errors in the following paragraphs, and replace them with the correct pronouns. Apply the rules of formal English usage. This exercise covers the rules in Chapters 17 and 18.

Us employees at Acme Manufacturing face a problem. The owner of our plant wants to hire new workers who will earn less money and have fewer benefits than us. Although the cuts in salary and benefits won't affect current employees like myself, we still object to the creation of a two-tier system. We think people who do the same jobs as us deserve the same pay. I personally think if the person next to me on the assembly line is getting paid less than me for the same job, this will create morale problems between him and I. He will constantly be asking the other workers and me, "Are you getting more per hour than me?"

The owner he doesn't care about morale problems among us employees. His concern is the bottom line. He says it is him who has to make the hard decisions and that he has to do what is in the best interest of the entire company. He says the other current employees and me should be grateful that we're not getting salary and benefit cuts ourselfs.

However, assembly line workers like me don't rely just on our regular salaries. We also earn extra money by working overtime hours. Let's say that a supervisor has to choose between giving overtime to me or to a new employee who earns three dollars less per hour than me. Would he choose the new employee or I? The answer is obvious. He'd look at the bottom line, and it would be me who wouldn't get the extra work.

I'm not sure what options us employees have right now. It's clear to the other current workers and I that we have a lot to lose if the company implements a two-tier system. I myself think we should call a meeting of all the workers to decide if there is any way that the owner and us can work out a better solution to the company's financial problems.

Chapter 19

Agreement of Pronouns with Their Antecedents

AGREEMENT IN NUMBER

Like nouns, pronouns may be either singular or plural, depending on whether they refer to one or more than one person or thing. Following are the subject, object, and possessive pronouns you have learned, divided into singular and plural categories.

Singular Pronouns

Subject	Object	Possessive	Possessive Adjectives
I	me	mine	my
you	you	yours	your
he	him	his	his
she	her	hers	her
it	it	its	its

Plural Pronouns

Subject	Object	Possessive	Possessive Adjectives
we	us	ours	our
you	you	yours	your
they	them	theirs	their

Just as a subject must agree in number with its verb, **a pronoun must agree in number with its antecedent.** (The **antecedent,** you will remember, is the noun to which the pronoun refers.) In other words, if the antecedent is *singular,* the pronoun must be *singular.* If the antecedent is *plural,* the pronoun must be *plural.*

Study the following sentences, in which both the pronouns and their antecedents have been italicized.

Because the *teacher* is ill, *she* will not be at school today.

Because the *teachers* are ill, *they* will not be at school today.

Obviously, few people would make pronoun agreement errors in the above sentences because *teacher* is clearly singular, and *teachers* is clearly plural. However, people often make pronoun agreement errors in cases like the following:

INCORRECT	If an airline *passenger* wants to be certain not to miss a flight, *they* should arrive at the airport an hour before the scheduled departure time.
CORRECT	If an airline *passenger* wants to be certain not to miss a flight, *he* should arrive at the airport an hour before the scheduled departure time.

Because *passengers* include females as well as males, it would be equally correct to say:

If an airline *passenger* wants to be certain not to miss a flight, *she* should arrive at the airport an hour before the scheduled departure time.

If an airline *passenger* wants to be certain not to miss a flight, *she* or *he* should arrive at the airport an hour before the scheduled departure time.

For a more detailed discussion of the *his* or *her* construction, see the section on "Avoiding Sexist Use of Pronouns" on page 192.

Notice the differences in these sentences:

INCORRECT	Each *student* brought *their* notebook.
CORRECT	Each *student* brought *his* notebook.

What causes people to make mistakes like these? The mistakes may occur because when a writer describes a *passenger,* she is thinking of *passengers* (plural) in general. Similarly, a writer may think of a *student* as *students* in general. Nevertheless, because *passenger* and *student* are singular nouns, they must be used with singular pronouns.

Notice that if several pronouns refer to the same antecedent, all of the pronouns must agree in number with that antecedent.

Before *Mike* begins to run, *he* always stretches *his* muscles.

If the *students* don't review *their* lessons, *they* won't do well on *their* final exams.

Another common pronoun agreement error involves **indefinite pronouns.** As you learned in Chapter 6 on subject–verb agreement, indefinite pronouns are *singular* and require *singular* verbs. (For example, "Everyone *is* happy," *not* "Everyone *are* happy.") Similarly, when indefinite pronouns are used as antecedents, they require *singular* subject, object, and possessive pronouns.

The following words are singular indefinite pronouns:

anybody, anyone, anything

each, each one

either, neither

everybody, everyone, everything

nobody, no one, nothing

somebody, someone, something

Notice the use of *singular pronouns* with these words:

Everyone did as *he* pleased.

Somebody has forgotten *her* purse.

Either of the choices has *its* disadvantages.

In informal spoken English, plural pronouns are often used with indefinite pronoun or adjective antecedents. However, this construction is generally not considered appropriate in formal speech or writing.

| INFORMAL | *Somebody* should let you borrow *their* book. (adjective) |
| FORMAL | *Somebody* should let you borrow *his* book. (adjective) |

In some sentences, an indefinite pronoun is so clearly plural in meaning that a singular pronoun sounds awkward with it. For example,

Everyone on this block must be wealthy because *they* all drive a Lexus or a Mercedes-Benz.

A better wording for this sentence would be:

The people on this block must be wealthy because they all drive a Lexus or a Mercedes-Benz.

AVOIDING SEXIST USE OF PRONOUNS

Although matching singular pronouns with singular antecedents is a grammatical problem, a usage problem may occur if the antecedent of a singular pronoun refers to both genders. In the past, singular masculine pronouns were used to refer to antecedents such as *worker* or *student* even if these antecedents included women as well as men. Now, writers prefer to use forms that include both sexes, such as *he* or *she* or *his* or *her* to avoid excluding women.
Notice the difference between the first sentence below and its revisions.

A good doctor always treats *his* patients with respect.

This sentence suggests that all doctors are men. The sentence *must* be revised by substituting a plural noun and pronoun or adjective.

Good doctors always treat *their* patients with respect.

It is also possible to rewrite the sentence so that it no longer contains a possessive.

Good doctors always treat patients with respect.

How could you reword the following sentence so that it includes both men and women?

Every soldier who is injured in combat is entitled to free medical care for his injuries.

AGREEMENT IN PERSON

In grammar, pronouns are classified into groups called **persons. First person** refers to the person who is speaking. **Second person** refers to the person being spoken to. **Third person** refers to the person or thing being spoken about. Below is a chart of subject pronouns grouped according to person.

	Singular	*Plural*
First person	I	we
Second person	you	you
Third person	he, she, it	they

All nouns are considered third person (either singular or plural) because nouns can be replaced by third-person pronouns (for example, *Susie* = *she*; *a car* = *it*; *babysitters* = *they*).

Just as a pronoun and its antecedent must agree in number, they must also agree in person. Agreement in person becomes a problem only when the second-person pronoun *you* is incorrectly used with a third-person antecedent. Study the following examples:

INCORRECT	If *anyone* wants to vote, *you* must be on the voters' list.
CORRECT	If *anyone* wants to vote, *he* or *she* must be on the voters' list.
INCORRECT	When *drivers* get caught in a traffic jam, *you* become impatient.
CORRECT	When *drivers* get caught in a traffic jam, *they* become impatient.

This type of mistake is called a **shift in person** and is considered a serious grammatical error.

In addition to avoiding shifts in person within individual sentences, you should try to be consistent in your use of person when you are writing essays. In general, an entire essay is written in the same person. If, for example, you are writing an essay about the special problems faced by students who work full time, you will probably use either the first or the third person. You should avoid shifts into the second person (*you*) because *you* refers to the reader of your paper and not to the students you are writing about.

INCORRECT	*Students* who work full time have special concerns. For example, *you* must arrange *your* classes to fit *your* work schedule.
CORRECT	*Students* who work full time have special concerns. For example, *they* must arrange *their* classes to fit *their* work schedule.

▶ Circle the pronoun that correctly completes each sentence.

The zoo has extended its hours so that patrons may visit when (your, his, their) schedules allow.

Participants must bring tickets to the front office, or else (you, he, they) will forfeit (your, his, their) chance to win the free gift.

Pay close attention; (your, his, their) final exam grade depends on following the directions carefully.

EXERCISE 19A

▶ If a sentence contains a pronoun error, cross out the incorrect pronoun and write in the correct form. Some sentences may contain more than one error. If a sentence contains no pronoun errors, label it C for *correct*. Apply the rules of formal English usage. Sentences 1–10 cover only the rules from Chapter 19.

1. Each of the women on the tennis team won their first game.

2. All club members need to bring your membership cards to the conference.

3. Neither of those restaurants has vegetarian entrees on their menu.

4. Every working mother needs reliable childcare for their children.

5. If anyone disagrees with this proposal, they must speak up now.

6. Has someone forgotten their briefcase?

7. Either my brother or my brother-in-law will let me use his car.

8. If a student plans to drop out of school, you should talk with your counsellor first.

9. Everyone must plan our own exercise program.

10. Does every student have their papers ready to turn in?

▶ The following sentences cover rules from Chapters 17–19.

11. The professor gave Natasha and I the two best grades in the class.

12. Irene bakes cakes and pastries better than me.

13. Imtiaz and Aysha brought goodbye gifts for you and I.

14. Us neighbours must band together to stop the speeders on our street.

15. My father, he always loves to tell stories to my brother and I about his life in Europe.

16. Be sure to tell her and them about the new mall downtown.

17. If it were up to me, everyone would have their birthday on the weekend so they could have time to celebrate!

18. If anyone wants some pop, you can take a glass and get some now.

19. My English professor made Parker and I an offer we couldn't refuse.

20. Us students are able to choose our own composition topics.

EXERCISE 19B

▶ If a sentence contains a pronoun error, cross out the incorrect error, and write in the correct pronoun. If a sentence contains no errors, label it C for *correct*. Sentences 7 and 20 should be reworded so that they do not refer exclusively to men. Apply the rules of formal English usage. This exercise covers rules from Chapters 17–19.

1. If anyone wants to buy a ticket to tonight's concert, they must be in line by noon.

2. My friend paid much more than me for his ticket because he chose a front-row seat.

3. If students want to enroll in an engineering class, you must first pass a math test.

4. Neither of these companies provides health coverage for their employees.

5. Our neighbours don't own as many cars as us.

6. If a person wants to vote in the United States, they must register at least thirty days before the election.

7. Every intelligent person knows he should not make a decision without carefully considering its consequences.

8. It is us consumers who decide whether or not a new product will be successful.

9. We offered to help our neighbours paint their house, but they decided to do the job themselfs.

10. If a customer wants to get the best sale merchandise, you should be at the store when the doors open.

11. It is up to you and I to decide what to do next.

12. Anyone who is pregnant should not get an X-ray unless her doctor believes it is absolutely necessary.

13. Please take the seat between Jim and I.

14. Each contest winner will have their name published in the local newspaper.

15. All the food for the party was prepared by my husband and myself.

16. Did you think that my roommate and me were making too much noise yesterday?

17. I always treat my friend to lunch because I earn much more money than her.

18. My daughter works in a bank, and my son, he manages a restaurant.

19. Geoff hurt himself while he was skiing last week.

20. If a person wants to be successful in business, he should find a mentor to guide his career.

Order of Pronouns
and Spelling of Possessives

ORDER OF PRONOUNS

When you are referring to someone else and to yourself in the same sentence, mention the other person's name (or the pronoun that replaces the name) before you mention your own.

INCORRECT	*I* and *Hans* are brothers.
CORRECT	*Hans* and *I* are brothers.
INCORRECT	You can borrow five dollars from *me* or *her*.
CORRECT	You can borrow five dollars from *her* or *me*.

The construction is actually not a rule of grammar; rather, it is considered a matter of courtesy.

Possessive Pronouns

Here is a list of possessive pronouns and their adjectives that you have already studied. This time, look carefully at how they are spelled and punctuated.

	Singular	*Plural*
First person	my, mine	our, ours
Second person	your, yours	your, yours
Third person	his	their, theirs
	her, hers	
	its	

Possessive pronouns do not contain apostrophes.

INCORRECT	The beach blanket was her's.
CORRECT	The beach blanket was hers.

Be especially careful not to confuse the possessive pronoun *its* with the contraction *it's* (it is).

INCORRECT	The car wouldn't start because *it's* battery was dead.
CORRECT	The car wouldn't start because *its* battery was dead.

Another source of confusion is the apostrophe, which indicates the omitted letters in contractions. For example, the apostrophe in *don't* represents the missing o from *do not*. Some contractions of pronouns and verbs have the same pronunciations as certain possessive pronouns. These pairs of words sound alike but differ in meaning. Don't confuse them in your writing.

who's–whose

Who's he? = *Who is* he?
Whose magazine is this? (possessive)

you're–your

You're looking well. = *You are* looking well.
Your car has a flat tire. (possessive)

they're–their

They're coming to the party. = *They are* coming to the party.

Their exhibit won the prize. (possessive)

(Note: *there* = *in that place, an adverb not a pronoun.*)

▶ Circle the pronoun that correctly completes each sentence.

That dog is (hers, her's).

(Whose, Who's) car is blocking the driveway?

The team just received (its, it's) award.

(Your, You're) a happy person.

The new house is (theirs, their's).

A final note: When you do pronoun exercises, or when you use pronouns in your own writing, remember to apply the rules you have learned. If you rely on what "sounds right," your instincts may supply only those pronouns that would be appropriate in *informal* English.

EXERCISE 20A

▶ If a sentence contains a pronoun error, cross out the incorrect pronoun and write in the correct form. Some sentences may contain more than one error. If a sentence contains no pronoun errors, mark it C for *correct*. Apply the rules of formal English usage. Sentences 1–10 cover only the rules from Chapter 20.

1. Its just not fair that it rains whenever we want to have a picnic.

2. Whose the best player on the team?

3. We promised to spend time with them on they're farm.

4. I and my best friend at work are competing for a promotion.

5. Mr. McAllister's unexpected death left its mark on every member of his family.

6. The guests were supposed to arrive by 7 o'clock, but their late.

7. Its commonly understood that your entitled to at least two coffee breaks each day.

8. I don't know who's dog that is because it's identification tag is missing.

9. Our class project won more prizes than their's in the science fair.

10. Your's is clearly the best entry in the contest.

▶ Sentences 11–20 cover rules from Chapters 17–20.

11. Everyone agrees that you and Tai make a better team than them.

12. Please help my friends and I to understand what we need to do next.

13. Julia and myself love to shop at this store because it's prices are so reasonable.

14. Don't do that job because its her's, not yours's.

15. Their just about the kindest people me and my family have ever known.

16. You're correct in thinking that I love to swim more than he.

17. Us campers must first put up our tents before we embark on a hike.

18. Our's is the tent with the huge blue circle on it's front.

19. We should make sure the person whose handling this project is the one who's skills are best suited for the job.

20. Every student needs to turn in their report by the last day of the month.

EXERCISE 20B

▶ If a sentence contains a pronoun error, cross out the incorrect pronoun, and write in the correct form. Some sentences may contain more than one error. If a sentence contains no pronoun errors, label it C for *correct*. Apply the rules of formal English usage. This exercise covers Chapters 17–20.

1. I don't know whose responsible for finishing this project.

2. I and my sisters are planning to take a vacation together this summer.

3. Those dishes aren't mine, so they must be your's.

4. That dog lowers it's tail when its getting ready to attack.

5. Are any passengers carrying luggage that isn't theirs?

6. If I were as wealthy as her, I'd quit work and travel around the world.

7. I don't know who's car caused the accident.

8. I know that you've been ill lately, but your looking very well today.

9. If students want to enroll for the fall semester, you must pay your fees by next week.

10. Anyone who is receiving financial aid should see their counsellor first.

11. Our children's school wants my husband and I to attend next week's open house.

12. A member of the women's track team was disqualified because they failed to pass the drug test.

13. My sisters are better athletes than I.

14. Our neighbours say their asking friends of theirs' to help them paint their house.

15. Those documents need to be signed by either Marta or me.

16. We pay more for automobile insurance than our neighbours because we have newer cars than them.

17. It's up to we parents to make sure our children know the dangers of smoking.

18. Can we remodel our kitchen ourselfs, or should we hire a contractor to do the work?

19. Hiring a contractor is more expensive, but a professional can do the job better and more quickly than us.

Unit 5 Review

▶ **Part 1:** Correct any pronoun errors in the following paragraphs. Cross out the incorrect pronouns, and write in the correct forms. Apply the rules of formal English usage.

Having a teenage driver in the family can be a stressful experience for we parents. Until this year, our son needed either my husband or I to drive him wherever he needed to go. Now that he is sixteen, it's important to him and his classmates to be able to drive by themselfs.

If a teenager wants to drive, they must first apply for a learner's permit. Our son studied the driver's handbook, and then my husband and myself took turns asking him questions about the driving rules. It turned out that our son knew the information better than us.

After he passed the written test, he then had to learn to drive. His high school used to offer driver's training classes, but the school had to cancel the classes because of reductions in it's budget. Some parents are sending their children to private driving schools, but they must have more money than us. We decided to teach our son to drive ourselfs. My husband did most of the teaching because he's a lot more patient than me. I'm the type of person whose easily upset in stressful situations, and my son says I make him nervous.

The only thing our son had difficulty with was parallel parking, but that's a problem for most people when you first learn to drive. Our son practised until he could park perfectly. He was worried about passing the test because his friends told him the driving examiners grade especially hard when their testing teenagers.

Fortunately, our son passed the driving test on his first try. However, I and my husband still set limits on his driving. He's not allowed to have more than one other person in the car with him at a time, and we limit the distance he's allowed to drive at night. After all, it's us who are paying for his insurance!

▶ **Part 2:** To make sure that you can use pronouns correctly, write the following kinds of sentences:

1. Write a sentence with a comparison using *than* and a **subject pronoun.**

_____

2. Write a sentence with a comparison using *than* and an **object pronoun.**

_____

3. Write a sentence that has two subjects: a **noun** and a **subject pronoun.**

_____

4. Write a sentence that has two direct objects or a preposition with two objects: a **noun** and an **object pronoun.**

_____

5. Write a sentence about yourself using the pronoun *myself* correctly.

_____

6. Write a sentence containing the pronoun *everyone* as a subject and a **possessive pronoun** agreeing in number with *everyone.*

_____

7. Write a sentence using both *you're* and *your.*

_____

8. Write a sentence using *who's.*

_____

9. Write a sentence using *whose.*

_____

10. Write a sentence using both *its* and *it's.*

_____

Unit 6

Capitalization, Additional Punctuation, Placement of Modifiers, Parallel Structure, and Irregular Verbs

Capitalization

The general principle behind capitalization is that **proper nouns** (names of *specific* persons, places, or things) are capitalized. **Common nouns** (names of *general* persons, places, or things) are *not* capitalized.

Study the following sentences, each of which illustrates a rule of capitalization.

1. Capitalize all parts of a person's name.

   That man is *John Allen Ford.*

2. Capitalize the titles of relatives only when the titles precede the person's name or when they take the place of a person's name.

   Our favourite relative is *Uncle Max.*

   Are you ready, *Mother?*

   but

   My *m*other and *f*ather are retired.

The same rule applies to professional titles.

We saw *Doctor Dhawan* at the market.

but

I must see a *doctor* soon.

3. Capitalize the names of streets, cities, and provinces.

Deirdre moved to 418 *River Drive*, *Coverdale*, *New Brunswick*.

4. Capitalize the names of countries, languages, and ethnic groups.

The two languages spoken most frequently in *Switzerland* are *German* and *French*, but some *Swiss* also speak *Italian*.

Poutine is a calorie-laden *French-Canadian* snack.

The Taj Mahal is a marvellous *Indian* monument to a man's love.

5. Capitalize the names of specific buildings, geographical features, schools, and other institutions.

They visited the *Tower of London*, the *Thames River*, and *Cambridge University*.

6. Capitalize the days of the week, the months of the year, and the names of holidays. Do not capitalize the names of the seasons of the year.

Monday, *February* 14, is *Valentine's Day*.

My favourite time of the year is the *fall*, especially *November*.

7. Capitalize directions of the compass only when they refer to specific regions.

Her accent revealed that she had been brought up in the *South*.

Edmonton is *north* of Calgary.

8. Capitalize the names of companies and brand names but not the names of the products themselves.

General Foods Corporation manufactures *Yuban* coffee.

We love *Tim Hortons'* donuts.

9. Capitalize the first word of every sentence.

10. Capitalize the subject pronoun I.

11. Capitalize the first word of a title and all other words in the title except for articles (a, an, the) and except for conjunctions and prepositions that have fewer than five letters.

    I really enjoyed the novel *Lives of Girls and Women* by Alice Munro.

    I enjoy reading the short essay "*Once More to the Lake.*"

12. Capitalize the names of academic subjects only if they are already proper nouns or if they are common nouns followed by a course number.

    Her schedule of classes includes *calculus*, *English*, and *Psychology* 101.

13. Capitalize the names of specific historical events, such as wars, revolutions, religious and political movements, and specific eras.

    The *Roaring Twenties* came to an end with the start of the *Depression*.

    Martin Luther was a key figure in the *Protestant Reformation*.

    My grandfather was wounded at *Juno Beach* during the *Second World War's D-Day* battles.

Exercise 21A

▶ Add capital letters to the following sentences wherever they are necessary.

1. Guided by our canadian automobile association mapbook, our family took a road trip across canada several years ago.

2. We travelled west with our neighbours, the smalls, through northern ontario, manitoba, saskatchewan, alberta, and british columbia, all the way to the pacific rim national park.

3. The great adventure began july 15 and ended august 25 after my children's birthdays.

4. We marvelled at how large our own province of ontario was as we spent several days camping and driving around lake superior across to kenora on the magnificent lake of the woods.

5. A visit to the alfalfa farm of a friend, harvey pentaman, near erickson, manitoba, showed us a whole new way of life.

6. Passing through the small manitoban town of neepawa reminded me of novelist margaret laurence's imaginary town manawaka, especially in *a jest of god*, which was made into the movie *rachel, rachel* directed by paul newman and starring joanne woodward.

7. The restful, flat drive through saskatchewan's prairies was made interesting by a visit to the training academy for the royal canadian mounted police in regina.

8. banff and jasper national parks in alberta are world famous for their incredible mountain scenery, wildlife, and the columbia icefields, but the children, daniella, stefan, ian, and kevin, were more fascinated by the badlands of drumheller, alberta.

9. Known as "the dinosaur capital of the world," this unesco world heritage site has colourful geological formations called hoodoos, and the royal tyrell museum.

10. We couldn't drag the kids away from the wonderful displays featuring, among others, tyrannosaurus rex and, of course, albertosaurus; it was like being in the film *jurassic park*.

11. Operated by the government of alberta, under the ministry of community development, the museum has attracted over half a million visitors each year since it opened in september, 1985.

12. When we visited friends, the wades, in edmonton, we finally slept in real beds rather than our tents, and headed to the world's largest indoor mall complex, the west edmonton mall.

13. We bought tickets to so many attractions that it was a very expensive day, with galaxyland amusement park and its rollercoaster, the walk-in aquariums of sea life caverns, and world waterpark with huge water slides and wave pool, not to mention eating at the food court's swiss chalet, a&w, and harveys.

14. Camping near kelowna on the beautiful okanagan lake in british columbia, we stayed up late to enjoy a meteor shower on my son stefan's birthday, august 12.

15. vancouver's stanley park, with its aquarium, and the suspension bridge at nearby capilano were exciting stops that inspired my daughter daniella to write a story, "under the sea and over the river," which she would later rewrite to gain admission into communications 101 at the university of western ontario.

16. When we took the ferry to victoria, vancouver island, we lost track of our neighbours, the smalls, who had taken the earlier boat.

17. Reunited, we explored the ancient and endangered rain forest of clayoquot sound, and then triumphantly waded into the ocean at pacific rim national park.

18. We had managed to experience much of what western canada has to offer, and when we got home to unionville, ontario, the children asked, "when can we do that again?"

EXERCISE 21B

▶ Add capital letters to the following paragraphs wherever they are needed.

my aunt barbara teaches english and speech at city central college in vancouver, british columbia. I often visit her there during the christmas holidays or during my summer vacation. One of the things I look forward to is having lunch or dinner with my aunt at one of the restaurants across the street from the college on forest drive. There is a chinese restaurant called fat guy. It specializes in the cuisine of the szechuan region with its hot pots. Because it caters mainly to students, it is open only on weekdays and closes on saturday and sunday. Whenever i go to the restaurant, I pick up a copy of the local mandarin and english newspaper, *ni hao,* which is in a rack by the front door. I also enjoy discussing chinese canadian literature with the restaurant's owner. His favourite novel is *disappearing moon café* by sky lee.

Of course, vancouver, like most of the pacific northwest, also has fine seafood restaurants. Fresh seafood from the pacific ocean is something that is usually hard for me to get because my home is in gimli, manitoba, and the only body of water near my home is lake winnipeg. Just a block north of city central college is a seafood restaurant called stone wall harbour. I especially enjoy eating the tiny oysters that are found only in olympia, washington. The original owner immigrated from england just after the second world war, and the restaurant's walls are still covered with photos of famous british landmarks, like buckingham palace, westminster abbey, and oxford university. In addition to serving very good seafood, the restaurant offers beverages imported from great britain, like bailey's irish tea, idris ginger beer, and guinness ale.

my next visit to my aunt will be during the weekend before the first of july. I plan to arrive early on friday morning so that I can attend an afternoon class, economics 107. The professor, dr. robert farrell, will be lecturing on a topic of special interest to me, the north american free trade agreement (NAFTA) and its effects on the economies of the united states, canada, and mexico.

Additional Punctuation

INTRODUCTORY MATERIAL

In Chapter 10 you learned to put a comma after an introductory dependent clause. At certain other times, it is customary to separate other *introductory* material from an independent clause that follows it.

> *At exactly 9:00* A.M., the meeting began. (introductory prepositional phrase)
>
> *After landing at the airport,* the plane sat on the runway for an hour. (introductory participial phrase)
>
> *Frightened by the noise,* the children ran to their parents. (introductory participial phrase)

COORDINATE ADJECTIVES

It is also customary to separate coordinate adjectives modifying the same noun. (Adjectives are *coordinate* if you can substitute *and* for the comma.)

They own a *small, cozy* cottage.

or

They own a small and cozy cottage.

DASHES

You learned in earlier lessons to use commas to set off appositives and parenthetical expressions. However, when the writer wishes to emphasize the importance or abruptness of such words, a **dash** may be used instead.

February—or maybe March—will be our last practice examination.

The prosecution's main witness—the defendant's own sister—will testify tomorrow.

COLONS

The **colon** is sometimes confused with the semicolon because of the similarity in names, but the two marks function differently. In addition to the colon's mechanical use to separate hours from minutes (8:45) and biblical chapters from verses (Genesis 2:5), this mark is frequently used to introduce lists, summaries, series, and quotations that may be of almost any length or form. (Notice that what follows the colon is not necessarily an independent clause; that is, it may be a fragment.) Lists or series of individual words or phrases begin with a lowercase, unless proper nouns.

He is studying three of the major Canadian novelists: Margaret Atwood, Carol Shields, and Alice Munro.

Two things are certain in life: death and taxes.

Shakespeare said it so well: "To thine own self be true."

When there is a complete sentence or more than one sentence introduced by the colon, use a capital letter to begin that sentence.

The conference dealt with several important issues: Industrial pollution is widening the hole in the ozone layer, the polar icecap is melting much faster than anticipated, and global warming is creating significant climate change.

APOSTROPHES

An **apostrophe** with an -*s* (*'s* or *s'*) in nouns and indefinite pronouns makes those words possessive. For singular nouns or indefinite pronouns, add the apostrophe followed by -*s*.

Dana's games

the dog's dish

everyone's responsibility

a day's effort

Shirley and Mario's cottage

or

Shirley's and Mario's cottage

For most plural nouns (those ending in an -*s*, -*sh*, or -*z* sound), use the apostrophe alone.

five cents' worth

the Phillips' house

the ladies' room

But for a plural noun not ending in an -*s*, -*sh*, or -*z* sound, add *'s*.

men's issues

children's toys

Sometimes possession is indicated by both the apostrophe and *of* in a prepositional phrase.

That CD *of* John's is my favourite.

And a possessive may also follow the word it modifies.

Is this CD John's?

DIRECT QUOTATIONS

Direct quotations make writing vivid. Long direct quotations as in research papers are indented and single spaced, but most direct quotes are simply enclosed in **quotation marks.**

"Just watch me!"

If the quotation is part of a longer sentence, it is set off by commas.

Pierre Elliott Trudeau said, "Just watch me!"

"Friends," the speaker said, "it's time for a new beginning."

Three rules govern the use of quotation marks with other forms of punctuation:

1. The comma and period are always placed *inside* the quotation marks.

   The class read "Fern Hill," a poem by Dylan Thomas.

2. The colon and semicolon are always placed *outside* the quotation marks.

   I love the song "Straight from the Heart"; it was recorded by Bryan Adams.

3. Question marks, exclamation marks, and dashes are placed *inside* the quotation marks if they apply only to the quoted material and *after* the quotation marks if they apply to the whole sentence.

   "Is dinner almost ready?" asked Beth.

   Did Shakespeare say, "The ripeness is all"?

QUOTATION MARKS VERSUS ITALICS

You may have noticed in the discussion of capitalization that some titles are punctuated with quotation marks ("Once More to the Lake"), and some titles are shown in *italics* (*Lives of Girls and Women*). The choice between these two ways to indicate titles is generally based on the length of the work. The titles of short works, such as songs, short poems and stories, essays and articles in periodicals, and episodes of a series, are put between *quotation marks*. The titles of longer works, such as full-length books and the names of newspapers, magazines, movies, television shows, and the titles of complete volumes or complete series, are put in *italics*.

Italics are a special slanted typeface used by printers. In a handwritten or typewritten paper, italics must be indicated by **underlining.**

We read the chapter "No Name Woman" from Maxine Hong Kingston's *The Woman Warrior*.

She sang the song "Ice Cream" from the musical *Anne of Green Gables*.

Did you see the episode "The Bulletin Board" on the television series *Corner Gas*?

The Times Herald printed an article titled "A New You" on the way cloning may influence how we think about our identity.

EXERCISE 22A

▶ **Part 1:** Add commas, colons, dashes, quotation marks, apostrophes, and italics to the following sentences wherever they are needed. Use dashes to punctuate abrupt parenthetical expressions. Indicate italics by *underlining*.

1. We finished the project on time but just barely late yesterday afternoon.

2. I've decided on a number of ways to become more politically active volunteering at the election office, driving people to the polls, and voting myself.

3. Wasn't it John F. Kennedy who said Ask not what your country can do for you; ask what you can do for your country?

4. In Shakespeare's famous poem, Sonnet 18, the speaker asks Shall I compare thee to a summer's day?

5. The professors meeting was postponed because several faculty members couldn't attend.

6. The soft gentle strokes of our new kitten made us laugh.

7. Director Chris Landreth and Seneca College students' animated film Ryan was recently nominated for an Academy Award.

8. Charles Dickens novel Hard Times contains a chapter titled Coketown.

9. I've thought about majoring in several very different fields computer science, philosophy, or history.

10. Sylvias recent promotion a complete surprise to her comes with a hefty increase in salary.

11. When you turn in your blue book the professor said be sure your student identification number is written on the cover.

12. The mens gymnasium has more exercise equipment than the womens.

13. Wanting to qualify for the Olympics the bobsledders practised seven hours a day.

▶ **Part 2:** Punctuate the following paragraph by adding commas, dashes, quotation marks, apostrophes, and italics wherever they are needed. Use dashes to punctuate abrupt parenthetical expressions. Indicate italics by *underlining*.

I was proudly demonstrating my newly acquired driving skills to my family when my mother suddenly exclaimed Slow down! By making a right turn too quickly I had created a twisted mass of my family in the cars back seat. My younger sister was nearly in tears, and my brothers face had turned white. I decided I had the following choices to stop driving, to apologize and return home immediately, or just to continue as if nothing had happened. I had just read a magazine article titled Young Adults and the Perils of Driving, but I never thought I'd be the young adult causing anyones peril.

By coincidence, the very next day, the Toronto Stars lead editorial was Too Young to Drive? It quoted statistics showing that a teenage drivers chances of causing an accident were much greater than those of other drivers. The article attributed this higher accident rate to two main factors lack of driving experience and over-confidence. Still embarrassed by yesterdays driving mishap I had to admit that I agreed with the papers editorial position. However, I still think I'm usually a careful competent driver teenager or not!

EXERCISE 22B

▶ **Part 1:** Add the following punctuation marks to the sentences wherever they are needed: commas, colons, dashes, quotation marks, apostrophes, and italics. Use dashes to punctuate abrupt parenthetical expressions. Indicate italics by *underlining*.

1. The Indigenous Peoples of the Southwest raised three major crops corn, beans, and squash.

2. Under our parliamentary system it is possible for a candidate to become Prime Minister even if that person's party does not receive a majority of the popular vote.

3. My brother-in-law tells jokes all of them boring at every party he attends.

4. The number-one book on the Globe and Mails best-seller list for much of 2005 and 2006 was The Da Vinci Code.

5. Of all the features of our new house our favourite is our airy spacious living room.

6. David and Marthas favourite weekend activity is attending the city orchestras free outdoor concerts.

7. Responding to a question on whether he would invoke martial law during the 1970 October Crisis in Quebec, Trudeau said Just watch me!

8. Your planes departure time is 8:45 P.M.

9. There are two things you need to know about your new boyfriend he is already married, and his wife is suing him for thirty thousand dollars in unpaid child support.

10. A good days work is worth a decent days pay.

11. Do I need to bring a gift to the party asked Marie.

12. That won't be necessary the hostess replied because we are collecting money to buy a group gift.

13. The short story Trespasses appears in a book titled Runaway by Alice Munro.

14. Disturbed by reports of terrorist activity in the region the Allens decided to cancel their planned trip to Israel and Egypt.

15. The department store is having a sale on mens suits, womens shoes, and childrens toys.

16. Toward the end of the military funeral a bugler played Taps then rifles fired a final salute to the deceased soldier.

17. Charlies plans for spending his weekly allowance include buying a dollars worth of candy and getting a gift for his best friends birthday party.

18. Every child deserves to attend a school with clean well-equipped classrooms.

19. Our local elementary school it's right around the corner from us doesn't have a single drinking fountain that works.

20. I read an article in my newspapers financial section titled Are You Paying Too Much for Automobile Insurance?

21. Wasn't it Shakespeare who wrote To be or not to be that is the question?

22. That recipe of Paulettes for triple chocolate cake is a chocolate lovers dream come true.

▶ **Part 2:** The following paragraph contains both capitalization errors and errors involving the use of some of the following punctuation marks: commas, colons, dashes, quotation marks, italics, and apostrophes. Correct any errors you find. Indicate italics by *underlining*.

While I was reviewing for a final exam in my european History class, a book that helped me a lot was "Almanac of World History", published by the national geographic society. this book covers world history from 10,000 B.C.E. to the present. Although it covers the history of the entire world, it's clear concise table of contents made it easy for me to find the chapters I needed on particular aspects of European history, such as the renaissance and the age of enlightenment. I found the chapter titled Europes balance of power: 1702–1763 especially helpful in explaining a period that is very confusing at least to me, that is. I also liked the books many short biographies of famous people. In a chapter describing how britain lost its worldwide empire in the years following the second world war there is a biography of mohandas k. gandhi, who said Non-cooperation with evil is as much a sacred duty as cooperation with good. Other features in this book that are very helpful to students include the following full-colour maps, lists of notable events for each historical era, and hundreds of photographs depicting the people and events in each chapter.

Misplaced and Dangling Modifiers

Modifiers are words that are used to describe other words in a sentence. A modifier may be a single word, a phrase, or a clause. (Adjective clauses are discussed in Chapter 15.) Examples of some of the more common types of modifiers are given below. Circle the word that each italicized modifier describes.

ADJECTIVE	He drank a cup of *black* coffee.
ADJECTIVE CLAUSE	The woman *who is dressed in blue* is the bride's mother.
PREPOSITIONAL PHRASE	*With the help of a nurse*, the patient was able to take a shower.

The words you should have circled are *coffee*, which is modified by "black," *woman*, which is modified by "who is dressed in blue," and *patient*, which is modified by "with the help of a nurse."

Another type of modifier is a **participial phrase.** A participial phrase begins with a participle. A **participle** is a verb form that functions as an adjective. There are two kinds of participles. **Present participles** are formed by adding -*ing* to the main verb (for example, *walking, knowing, seeing*). **Past participles** are the verb forms that are used with the helping verb *have* (have *walked*, have *known*, have ▶ *seen*). Circle the word that each of the following participial phrases modifies.

Looking excited, the child begged for more presents.

The woman *dressed very expensively* is a famous model.

The words that you should have circled are *child* and *woman*.

If you look back at all the words that you have circled so far in this chapter, you will notice that although modifiers sometimes precede and sometimes follow the words they describe, they are in all cases placed as closely as possible to the word that they describe. Failure to place a modifier in the correct position in a sentence results in an error known as a **misplaced modifier.**

MISPLACED	He told a joke to his friends *that no one liked.* (Did no one like his friends?)
CORRECT	He told a joke *that no one liked* to his friends.
MISPLACED	Sandy always uses pencils for her math exams *with extremely fine points.* (Do the exams have extremely fine points?)
CORRECT	Sandy always uses pencils *with extremely fine points* for her math exams.

▶   Correct the misplaced modifiers in the following sentences.

The citizen informed the police officer that the thief had escaped by phone.

The child clutched the old teddy bear with tears rolling down his face.

A firm called Threshold provides companions for people who are dying at $7.50 per hour.

An error related to the misplaced modifier is the **dangling modifier.** A dangling modifier sometimes occurs when a participial phrase is placed at the beginning of a sentence. A participial phrase in this position *must describe the subject of the following clause.* If the subject of the clause cannot logically perform the action described in the participial phrase, the phrase is said to "dangle" (to hang loosely, without a logical connection).

DANGLING	While *typing a letter,* my contact lens popped out. (This sentence suggests that the *contact lens* was typing the letter.)
CORRECT	*While I was typing a letter,* my contact lens popped out.
DANGLING	*Trying to save money,* Trisha's clothes were bought at a thrift shop. (This sentence suggests that Trisha's *clothes* were trying to save money.)
CORRECT	Trying to save money, *Trisha* bought her clothes at a thrift shop.

Notice that there are several ways to correct dangling modifiers. You may add a noun or pronoun to the sentence to provide a word that the modifier can logically describe, or you may reword the entire sentence. *However, simply reversing the order of the dangling modifier and the rest of the sentence does not correct the error.*

DANGLING	*While sleeping,* her phone rang.
STILL DANGLING	Her phone rang *while sleeping.*
CORRECT	While she was sleeping, her phone rang.

► Revise the following sentences so that they no longer contain dangling modifiers.

After standing all day, my feet look forward to sitting down.

While vacuuming the carpet, the fuse blew.

While taking the final exam, my pen ran out of ink.

By eating well, your life will be prolonged.

Because misplaced and dangling modifiers create confusing and even absurd sentences, you should be careful to avoid them in your writing.

EXERCISE 23A

▶ **Part 1:** Rewrite the following sentences so that they do not contain misplaced or dangling modifiers. Some sentences may have more than one error. If a sentence has no modifier errors, mark it C for *correct*.

1. After cleaning her floor, the mop was put in the closet.

   _____

   _____

2. The lonely woman walked slowly down the street with a shuffling gait.

   _____

   _____

3. Wanting to ensure that the party went well, the hostess carefully planned every detail.

   _____

   _____

4. The bride looked beautiful as she walked down the aisle dressed in ivory silk chiffon.

   _____

   _____

5. The professor ordered his students with a loud voice to turn in their assignments.

   _____

   _____

6. After marrying the prince, the fairy tale ended happily ever after.

   _____

   _____

7. The man won the contest eating the most hot dogs.

   _____

   _____

8. While driving to the beach this summer, my car's transmission gave out.

_____

_____

9. I brought a present to the baby shower wrapped in pink and blue paper.

_____

_____

10. After playing ball with his dog, Robbie felt exhilarated.

_____

_____

▶ **Part 2:** Construct five sentences of your own, using the modifiers listed below in the positions indicated in the sentences. Make certain that your modifiers are not misplaced and are not dangling.

11. While jogging yesterday afternoon, _____.

12. After practising his guitar, _____.

13. _____ that had won the fair's pastry contest.

14. After singing in the church choir, _____.

15. _____ while listening to his MP3 player.

EXERCISE 23B

▶ **Part 1:** Some of the following sentences contain misplaced modifiers or dangling modifiers. Rewrite these sentences. If a sentence is already correctly constructed, label it C for *correct*.

1. Not being familiar with the freeway, our car exited at the wrong off-ramp.

   _____

   _____

2. I put some tomatoes in the refrigerator for my salad.

   _____

   _____

3. To be considered for the job, your application form must include three references.

   _____

   _____

4. This restaurant offers meals at half-price to customers who are senior citizens from 5 to 6 P.M.

   _____

   _____

5. Wanting to be picked up and carried, the baby began to cry.

   _____

   _____

6. The hostess served raw oysters to her guests on the half-shell.

   _____

   _____

7. After handling fish, a slice of lemon will remove the fish's odour from your hands.

   _____

   _____

8. I bought a sweater in a thrift shop that cost only three dollars.

_____

_____

9. At the age of sixteen, my father bought me my first car.

_____

_____

10. I made a birthday cake for my daughter's party with chocolate cream frosting and a strawberry filling.

_____

_____

▶ **Part 2:** Correct any misplaced or dangling modifiers in the following paragraph.

While attending college, some of my instructors graded my papers very harshly. I remember one English teacher who gave a failing grade to any essay by a student with more than three spelling errors. I've always had trouble with spelling, and whenever writing compositions in class, my palms would begin to sweat. I was supposed to look up any word in the dictionary that was misspelled, but I couldn't always find the words I needed because, of course, I didn't know how to spell them in the first place. However, after buying an electronic spelling dictionary, my composition grades improved. When using the electronic dictionary, even incorrectly spelled entries would give me the correctly spelled word. I would recommend using an electronic dictionary for any student in any class with a spelling problem.

Parallel Structure

The term **parallel structure** means that similar ideas should be expressed in similar grammatical structures. For example, Benjamin Franklin quoted the following proverb:

Early to bed and early to rise make a man healthy, wealthy, and wise.

This proverb is a good illustration of parallel structure. It begins with two similar phrases, "Early to bed" and "early to rise," and it ends with a series of three similar words (they are all adjectives): *healthy, wealthy,* and *wise.*

In contrast, the following two versions of the same proverb contain some words that are *not* parallel.

Early to bed and early *rising* make a man healthy, wealthy, and wise.

Early to bed and early to rise make a man healthy, wealthy, and *give him wisdom.*

These last two sentences, therefore, are not properly constructed.

Because there are many different grammatical structures in the English language, the possibilities for constructing nonparallel sentences may appear to be almost unlimited. Fortunately, you do not have to be able to identify all the grammatical structures in a sentence to tell whether or not that sentence has parallel structure. Sentences that lack parallel structure are usually so awkward that they are easy to recognize.

NOT PARALLEL	My chores are *washing dishes, cleaning the bathrooms, and to water the lawn.*
PARALLEL	My chores are *washing dishes, cleaning the bathrooms,* and *watering the lawn.*
NOT PARALLEL	I expect you *to read all the assignments, to complete all the exercises, and that you should attend every class.*
PARALLEL	I expect you *to read* all the assignments, *to complete* all the exercises, and *to attend* every class.
NOT PARALLEL	The fortune teller said my husband would be *tall, dark, and have good looks.*
PARALLEL	The fortune teller said my husband would be *tall, dark,* and *good-looking.*

▶ Revise each of the following sentences so that it is parallel in structure.

The steak was tough, overcooked, and had no taste.

The school emphasizes the basic skills of reading, how to write, and arithmetic.

He spent his day off playing tennis and went to the beach.

Your blind date is attractive and has intelligence.

Some errors in parallel structure occur when a writer is not careful in the use of correlative conjunctions. **Correlative conjunctions** are conjunctions that occur in pairs, such as:

both . . . and

either . . . or

neither . . . nor

not only . . . but also

Because these conjunctions occur in pairs, they are usually used to compare two ideas. For example,

> My professor suggests that I *not only* study more *but also* attend class more regularly.

Correctly used, correlative conjunctions will structure a sentence in effective parallel form.

The rule for using correlative conjunctions is that the conjunctions *must be placed as closely as possible to the words that are being compared.* For example,

> I must go home *either* today *or* tomorrow.

> not

> I *either* must go home today *or* tomorrow.

Study the following examples of correctly and incorrectly placed correlative conjunctions.

INCORRECT	Stefan *not only* got an "A" in math *but also* in English.
CORRECT	Stefan got an "A" *not only* in math *but also* in English.
INCORRECT	Shirley *neither* is a good housekeeper *nor* a good cook.
CORRECT	Shirley is *neither* a good housekeeper *nor* a good cook.

▶ Correct the misplaced correlative conjunctions in the following sentences.

Bill both collects stamps and coins.

Shani neither eats meat nor dairy products.

Daniella both plays the piano and the flute.

My daughter not only has had chicken pox but also mumps.

EXERCISE 24A

▶ Rewrite any sentences that lack parallel structure. If a sentence is already parallel, label it C for *correct*.

1. Kurt loved to cook, to read mystery novels, and travelling to remote places.

   _____

   _____

2. Jim not only has mastered the guitar but also the piano.

   _____

   _____

3. Francesca is either going to the gym or the community pool.

   _____

   _____

4. After she graduated from college, Julia's goals were finding a new job, moving to a new apartment, and learning to cook.

   _____

   _____

5. Joe both bought a new computer and a new DVD player.

   _____

   _____

6. When I left for college, my parents told me to study hard, to choose my friends wisely, and that I should phone home at least once a week.

   _____

   _____

7. We want to create a position for someone who has imagination, energy, and who is enthusiastic.

   _____

   _____

8. Being fired from his job made Tomas bitter, angry, and a pessimist.

   _____

   _____

9. The actors not only practised their lines in the studio but also in front of a live audience.

_____

_____

10. To live on your own is a lot different from living with your parents.

_____

_____

11. The contestants were told to limit their program to ten minutes and that they should have a substitute program too.

_____

_____

12. We neither want you to stop studying nor to stop your sports activities.

_____

_____

13. I am going to listen to the professor, take good notes, and study every day.

_____

_____

14. This house is too small, too far from our jobs, and it costs too much.

_____

_____

15. Having a part-time job teaches high school students not only how to manage their money but also their time.

_____

_____

EXERCISE 24B

▶ Rewrite any sentences that lack parallel structure or that contain misplaced or dangling modifiers. If a sentence has no errors, label it C for *correct*.

1. Italy has beautiful scenery, delicious food, and people who are friendly.

   _____

   _____

2. The doctor advised the patient to stop smoking and that he should lose 13 kilograms.

   _____

   _____

3. The wedding dinner was very costly because the guests were not only served a five-course meal but also very expensive imported champagne.

   _____

   _____

4. After vacationing in Guatemala for a month, my Spanish improved a lot.

   _____

   _____

5. Because we are vegetarians, we neither eat meat nor dairy products.

   _____

   _____

6. Albert Einstein said that having imagination is more important than to have knowledge.

   _____

   _____

7. Her thumb was cut while chopping vegetables for dinner.

   _____

   _____

8. In speaking of a military victory, Julius Caesar said, "I came, I saw, I conquered."

   _____

   _____

9. Caesar's quotation in the original Latin (*Veni, vidi, vici*) not only has parallel structure but also alliteration.

   _____

   _____

10. My composition instructor said my essay needed a clearer thesis, more specific supporting details, and that its organization should be better.

    _____

    _____

11. While waiting for my flight to depart, a crossword puzzle helped me to pass the time.

    _____

    _____

12. If you win the lottery, you either get thirty million dollars paid over a twenty-year period or twelve million dollars in one lump sum.

    _____

    _____

13. I want to find a job that gives me a good salary, a chance to travel, and an adequate retirement plan.

    _____

    _____

14. The Thai restaurant serves skewers of meat to its guests with peanut sauce.

    _____

    _____

15. The mistakes people often make when they try to use chopsticks for the first time are holding them too close to the bottom and to move both sticks at the same time.

    _____

    _____

Irregular Verbs

Verbs have three **principal** (meaning "most important") **parts:** the *present* (which, when preceded by *to*, becomes the *infinitive*), the *past*, and the *past participle*.

The **present** form may stand alone as a main verb without any helping verb. For example,

I *like* movies.

We *watch* television each night.

It may also be preceded by a helping verb, such as *can, could, do, does, did, may, might, must, shall, should, will,* or *would.* (A list of helping verbs appears in Chapter 4.)

I *must talk* with you tomorrow.

Jennifer *should study* her vocabulary words.

However, the present form is not used after any forms of the helping verbs *have* (*has, have, had*) or *be* (*am, is, are, was, were, been*). The **past participle** (see below) is used after these verbs.

The **past** form is used alone as a main verb. It is *not* preceded by a helping verb when expressing the simple past tense.

They *ran* back to the classroom.

We *spelled* all the words correctly.

The **past participle** is preceded by at least one, and sometimes more than one, helping verb. The helping verb is often a form of *have* or *be*.

She *has spoken* very kindly of you.

The batter *was hit* by a ball.

Neil *had* always *been* poor until he won the lottery.

Most English verbs are **regular.** A regular verb forms both its past and past participle by adding *-ed* to the present. (If the present already ends in *-e*, only a *-d* is added.)

Present	*Past*	*Past Participle*
walk	walked	walked
live	lived	lived

Any verb that does *not* form both its past and past participle by adding *-ed* or *-d* is considered **irregular.** For example,

Present	*Past*	*Past Participle*
fall	fell	fallen
give	gave	given
hide	hid	hidden

Because irregular verbs by definition have irregular spellings, you must *memorize* the spelling of their past and past participle forms. Irregular verbs include many of the most commonly used verbs in the English language (for example, *come, go, eat, drink, sit, stand*), so it is important to study them carefully.

Several pairs of verbs are often confused: *lie/lay, sit/set,* and *rise/raise.*

The irregular verb *lie* means to recline or to be in a horizontal position.

I *lie* down whenever I feel dizzy.

The verb *lay* means to put something down. This verb always has a direct object.

Lay your cards on the table.

The hen *laid* six eggs.

(Notice that the verb *lie,* meaning to say something that is not true, is a *regular* verb: *lie, lied, lied.*)

The verb *sit* means to be in a seated position.

I always *sit* in the front row of a classroom.

One meaning of the verb *set* is to put something in a particular place. When it is used in this sense, *set* has a direct object.

She always *sets* her table with fine china and linen napkins.

He *set* the clocks an hour ahead last night.

The verb *rise* means to get up or go higher.

The audience *rose* to sing the national anthem.

The sun *rises* at seven A.M.

One meaning of the verb *raise* is to lift something higher or to increase it. When used in this sense, *raise* has a direct object.

After we *raise* the curtain, the performance will begin.

The store *raised* its prices after the sale ended.

The verb *raise* is regular: *raise, raised, raised.*

Here is a list of some of the most commonly used irregular verbs. In addition to learning the verbs on this list, if you are not sure whether or not a verb is irregular, look it up in the dictionary. A good dictionary will list the principal parts of an irregular verb in addition to defining its meaning.

Present	Past	Past Participle
beat	beat	beaten
begin	began	begun
bend	bent	bent
bleed	bled	bled

Present	*Past*	*Past Participle*
blow	blew	blown
break	broke	broken
bring	brought	brought
build	built	built
buy	bought	bought
catch	caught	caught
choose	chose	chosen
come	came	come
cut	cut	cut
do	did	done
draw	drew	drawn
drink	drank	drunk
drive	drove	driven
eat	ate	eaten
fall	fell	fallen
feed	fed	fed
feel	felt	felt
find	found	found
fly	flew	flown
freeze	froze	frozen
get	got	got *or* gotten
give	gave	given
go	went	gone
grow	grew	grown
have	had	had
hear	heard	heard
hide	hid	hidden
hit	hit	hit
hurt	hurt	hurt
keep	kept	kept
know	knew	known
lay	laid	laid

Present	*Past*	*Past Participle*
leave	left	left
lend	lent	lent
lie	lay	lain
lose	lost	lost
make	made	made
mean	meant	meant
meet	met	met
pay	paid	paid
put	put	put
read (say "reed")	read (say "red")	read (say "red")
ride	rode	ridden
ring	rang	rung
rise	rose	risen
run	ran	run
see	saw	seen
sell	sold	sold
send	sent	sent
set	set	set
shake	shook	shaken
shoot	shot	shot
sing	sang	sung
sink	sank	sunk
sit	sat	sat
sleep	slept	slept
speak	spoke	spoken
spend	spent	spent
spin	spun	spun
stand	stood	stood
steal	stole	stolen
stick	stuck	stuck
swear	swore	sworn
swim	swam	swum

Present	*Past*	*Past Participle*
take	took	taken
teach	taught	taught
tear	tore	torn
tell	told	told
think	thought	thought
throw	threw	thrown
wear	wore	worn
weep	wept	wept
win	won	won
write	wrote	written

Notice that compound verbs follow the same pattern as their root form. For example,

be*come*	be*came*	be*come*
for*give*	for*gave*	for*given*
under*stand*	under*stood*	under*stood*

Exercise 25A

▶ Fill each blank with the correct form (past or past participle) of the verb in parentheses. Try to do this exercise without looking at the list of verbs in your book.

1. (stick) She should have _____ to her usual routine.

2. (ride) Has he _____ horses for a long time?

3. (fall) Yesterday, I _____ off my horse three times.

4. (understand) Many of our classmates have not _____ this assignment.

5. (throw) The third baseman _____ the ball a lot better at last night's game.

6. (set) She had just _____ her packages down when the phone began to ring.

7. (ring) The phone had already _____ eight times before she could answer it.

8. (know) When I took the test yesterday, I thought I _____ the answers, but I didn't.

9. (read) She _____ the instructions three times before beginning to write.

10. (hurt) Falling off the beam _____ her chances of winning the competition.

11. (meet) When they first _____ each other, they knew they would become lifelong friends.

12. (swim) Last season, they _____ the course faster than anyone else.

13. (feel) My sisters have always _____ sad about leaving our hometown.

14. (drive) Demetrios _____ the car for the first time yesterday.

15. (catch) The pitcher _____ the ball and threw it to the first baseman.

16. (lay) As soon as she _____ the baby down, he began to cry.

17. (swear) My uncle _____ he was at the party last week, but we didn't see him.

18. (lie) After a long day at work yesterday, I _____ down for fifteen minutes.

19. (take) They have _____ far too long to repair my car.

20. (choose) The students _____ one person to represent them at the conference.

21. (grow) It was clear that he had _____ a great deal from his experience of living away from home.

22. (rise) The moon _____ slowly in the evening sky.

23. (pay) She was _____ well for all the good work she had done.

24. (feed) Had she _____ the children before they started to cry?

25. (sink) We watched in shock as the small boat slowly _____.

26. (win) One student _____ two prizes at the science fair last winter.

27. (write) They have _____ letters to each other for several years.

28. (steal) If he had not _____ that man's wallet, he would have been in law school today.

29. (keep) Although we asked her to stop, she _____ right on singing the same song over and over and over again.

30. (fly) As their plane _____ off, we realized how much we would miss our friends.

Exercise 25B

Grammar Note: The **past perfect tense** is formed by using the helping verb *had* plus the past participle of the main verb. The past perfect tense is used if you are already writing in the past tense and need to refer to an action that happened even earlier.

Milo ate very little at the party because he *had eaten* dinner just an

hour earlier.

The prisoner *had* already *served* ten years in prison when the governor

decided to pardon him.

▶ Fill each blank with the correct form (past or past participle) of the verb in parentheses.

Last night, our phone (ring)_____ at 2 A.M. My husband

and I had (go) _____ to bed three hours earlier, and we

had (fall) _____ asleep almost immediately. My husband

answered the phone, and as soon as I (hear) _____ his first

few words, I (know) _____ that the call (bring)

_____ bad news. It was from our eighteen-year-old

daughter, who had (leave) _____ home in September to

attend college in another province. I immediately (get)

_____ out of bed and (go)_____downstairs to pick

up another phone.

Our daughter (tell) _____ us that her roommate, Amy,

had been critically injured in an automobile accident only a few hours

earlier. She had (speak) _____with a police officer who had

(come) _____ to the apartment that she and Amy shared

with two other girls. The officer (think) _____ that Amy

might have been drinking because witnesses said she was driving erratically before her car (hit) _____ a tree on the side of the road and (catch) _____ fire. Fortunately, Amy was the only person who was (hurt)_____ in the accident.

Our daughter knew that Amy occasionally (drink) _____ a little, but, according to our daughter, Amy never (drive) _____ if she had been drinking. Amy always (make) _____ sure she (have) _____ a friend to drive her home before she (begin) _____ to drink.

Our daughter (weep) _____ as she talked to us. Amy had been so badly injured in the accident that she had almost (bleed)_____ to death before she was (take) _____ to the hospital. Both of her legs were (break) _____, and she had severe internal injuries as well as burns. Our daughter was calling us from the hospital. She had (go)_____ there in order to be near Amy. Even if there was nothing she could do to help Amy, she (feel) _____ that was where she needed to be.

My husband and I (find)_____ it impossible to go back to sleep. Instead, we (spend)_____ the rest of the night talking to each other and worrying about our daughter and Amy. We (keep) _____ imagining what Amy's parents were going through. When the sun (rise)_____ at 6:30 A.M., we (make) _____ a pot of coffee and (eat) _____ a little breakfast before we called our daughter and then (leave) _____ the house to go to work.

Unit 6 Review

▶ **Part 1:** Add capital letters to the following passage wherever they are needed.

Women's hockey in canada has come out of the shadows into the limelight. Our olympic team, team canada, was called "the most dominant team in women's hockey history" after its gold medal victory in salt lake city's winter games in 2002 and its sweep at the torino games in 2006.

Team coach melody davidson felt that the swedish team's upset victory over the american players in february 2006 at turin saved women's hockey. That was because team canada had been accused of "running up the score" mercilessly, due to the international ice hockey federation's scoring rules.

Our women's team had quickly defeated the italian, russian, and finnish teams, expecting to face the americans in the finals. The complaints about imbalance stopped when the swedes beat team usa and made the finals of the torino games much more exciting. Perhaps the swedes were inspired by their constant watching of the film *miracle*, in which the 1980 american men's hockey team was finally victorious over the russians.

When winger gillian apps put in the first goal of the final game in the 2006 olympics, the audience went wild. apps is the daughter of former nhl player syl apps, and her grandfather, syl apps senior, had been a hall of fame player, winner of the calder trophy and three stanley cups as a Toronto maple leaf.

The palasport olympico erupted when team canada won. The maple leaf was raised, "o canada" was played, and team canada was awarded the gold medal. Afterward, the women linked arms and sang "take me home, country roads," a song that had helped them bond. They had become the dominant force in women's hockey.

▶ **Part 2:** Some of the following sentences contain misplaced or dangling modifiers; others lack parallel structure. Rewrite the incorrect sentences. If a sentence has no structural errors, label it C for *correct*.

1. Before leaving for work, my children have to be dropped off at their preschool.

   _____

   _____

2. Preschools are necessary for parents of young children who work.

   _____

   _____

3. Why would you want to go to a restaurant that neither has good food nor reasonable prices?

   _____

   _____

4. We heard that the bank robber had been arrested on the evening news.

   _____

   _____

5. The real estate agent told me to paint my house, clean up my yard, and that I should repair my fence before I put my house up for sale.

   _____

   _____

6. I have a scar on my knee that is dark purple.

   _____

   _____

7. I can't believe that our boss expects so much work from so few people.

_____

_____

8. That house not only has a poor floor plan, but its space is inadequate also.

_____

_____

9. To qualify for this job, you need a college degree, at least three years' experience in a similar position, and be able to handle stressful situations.

_____

_____

10. Make sure that your car doesn't run out of gas while driving through the Yukon.

_____

_____

▶ **Part 3:** Add capital letters, commas, colons, dashes, apostrophes, quotation marks, and italics to the following passage wherever they are needed. Use dashes to punctuate abrupt parenthetical expressions. Indicate italics by *underlining*.

My sisters and I are planning a party for our parents 50th anniversary. We want to invite all of our relatives as well as my mother and fathers close friends. In planning a large party there are many factors to consider. First on our list of things to do was choosing the partys location. We wanted a large conveniently located site that had the following features ample parking, room for dancing, and wheelchair access. After days of discussion we finally reserved the ballroom of a local hotel.

Having chosen the site our next task was to choose a caterer and to decide on a menu. Choosing a caterer usually a very difficult decision was easy for us because our next-door neighbour, Ilya, owns a large catering business. Ilya said When you're preparing a dinner for seniors, you don't want to serve anything that's too exotic or that's hard to digest. Armed with suggestions from us about some of our parents favourite foods he had no trouble coming up with a meal that met all of his requirements and that was within our budgets limits too.

Our parents love to dance, and we wanted to play music from the 1950s. We found a book titled great songs of the 50s and 60s, and we used it to pick selections for the party. Of course, we included our parents favourite song, unchained melody. Our parents were so pleased when that song was revived during the 1990s because it was used as a theme for the movie ghost. Imagine hearing our song on the radio again they said. It's just like the good old days! Another of their favourite songs is that's all; we will play that song as the very last dance of the evening.

My sisters and I had so much fun planning this party that we're looking forward to our own golden anniversaries. Do you think I asked my sisters that all three of us will be lucky enough to have marriages that last fifty years? My sisters and I certainly hope so!

▶ **Part 4:** Fill each blank with the correct form (past or past participle) of the verb in parentheses.

The Heifer Project is a charity that helps needy families all over the world by giving them an animal to raise. If you find it difficult to imagine how the gift of a single animal can change a family's life, here is what can happen when a family receives the gift of a single cow.

Before the cow is (send) _____ to the family, the family members are (teach) _____ how to care for the animal. Careful instructions are (give) _____ about what the animal must be (feed) _____. If the animal needs to be (keep) _____ in a special shelter, that shelter must be (build) _____ before the animal arrives.

A cow is an especially valuable animal for a family because some of the milk it provides can be (drink) _____ by the family's children, and the rest can be (sell) _____ to earn the family extra money. Children in poor families are often small for their age because of insufficient protein in their diet, and many families have reported that their children suddenly (grow) _____ several inches after they (begin) _____ to drink milk every day.

The income from the sale of the milk can be (spend) _____ in a variety of ways. School fees can be (pay) _____ and uniforms can be (buy) _____ so that the children in the family will be able to attend school. Improvements may also be (make) _____ to the family's home. Sometimes a water-proof metal roof can replace one made of straw. Some families have even (build) _____ new homes with savings accumulated over the years.

Besides providing milk, the manure from the cow is used to fertilize the family's garden or field so that more crops can be (grow)

_____ and more food can be (eat) _____ at home or (take) _____ to the local market for sale there.

The Heifer Project has (hear) _____ from many recipients who have (write) _____ to thank donors for providing their animals and to describe what the gift of an animal has (mean) _____ to their families.

Unit 7

7

Paragraphs

Writing Effective Paragraphs

For many students, writing a formal essay can be an intimidating experience. It is not that writing itself is that distasteful. Writing e-mails, notes in class, poetry, or short stories can be fun and deeply satisfying. Sometimes, however, formal classroom assignments—paragraphs or essays—take all the fun out of writing, and it becomes hard.

Realistically, formal writing *is* hard. One writer told the truth when he joked, "Writing is easy. All you have to do is stare at the blank page until drops of blood appear on your forehead." Although we can't necessarily make academic writing a pleasure for everyone, we can help you gain understanding and mastery of its basic form, **the paragraph.**

Paragraphs are the foundational units of essays. If you can write effective paragraphs, chances are good that you'll be able to write effective essays. By understanding basic principles and mastering some fundamental structures and strategies, you can gain the control and confidence that can lead to more joy in writing.

WHAT'S A PARAGRAPH?

Everyone knows what a paragraph is. Paragraphs look a certain way. You look at a page and see lines of print or writing set off either by an indentation (as precedes the word "Paragraphs" of the following paragraph) or white spaces (as precedes and follows the heading "What's a Paragraph?"). When we see a paragraph, we have certain expectations. We expect that a new idea will follow, and we briefly rest our eyes and minds in the white space or indentation preceding this new idea. Consider how silently grateful you are when after reading a long, complex paragraph, you come to the white space that marks its end. Imagine how you might feel if an entire book had no paragraphs, but was solid text. *Paragraphs are visual units.*

Paragraphs carry meaning. When we see the white space and indentation, we recognize that the sentences in the group that follows relate to one another and focus on a particular idea. This idea is called **the topic sentence or main idea** of the paragraph. We will return to topic sentences later, but for now it is important to understand that *paragraphs are semantic units; that is, they convey ideas.*

Finally, a paragraph can communicate and carry meaning by its very size and placement. A one- or two-sentence paragraph will catch your attention, tell you something important, or indicate a change in the course of an argument. *Paragraphs are rhetorical units; that is, they influence and guide the reader by their very size and placement.*

EXERCISE A

▶ Break up the following sentences into paragraphs. Be able to explain your decisions. Do your new paragraphs each have a particular idea or focus?

My new car has made me very happy. I love its colour. It is a beautiful deep green with beige leather interior. It also has wonderful chrome rims that shine like silver. My car not only is pretty, it also is fast. It has 270 horsepower and can go up to 230 kilometres an hour. I have a sunroof, too. On bright, beautiful days, I open it so I can feel the warmth of the sun and the wind blowing in my hair. But what I really love about my car is its CD player and stereo system. I can play all my favourite music as I drive to work and school. I simply love my new car! My job makes me crazy. I work at a pizza place with three other people. Sometimes I think I'm the only one who is working. Yesterday, the other employees were "cleaning up" and left me with a ton of customers. I had to take their orders, bake their pizzas, cut them up, serve them to the customers, and work the cash register—all by myself. My job is straining my sanity.

CONTROLLING PRINCIPLES: UNITY AND COHERENCE

Understanding the two underlying principles of paragraphs (and essays) will help you to master formal writing.

Unity

The first principle, **unity,** means that *everything in your paragraph exists to explain, describe, illustrate, prove, discuss* **one point: your topic sentence or main idea.**

Your topic sentence or main idea is the purpose of your paragraph, the reason it exists. All the sentences in your paragraph *must directly relate* to your topic sentence. If they do not, your paragraph does not have **unity,** and it will sound like a jumble of ideas.

In the exercise above, you probably were able to notice at least two paragraphs. The first few sentences all dealt with one subject: my new car. The main idea of that paragraph is the exercise's first sentence, "My new car makes me very happy." Every sentence in that initial paragraph *relates directly* to the topic sentence. A new subject and paragraph begin with the sentence, "My job makes me crazy." The remainder of the sentences all *relate directly* to this one idea. These two paragraphs each have unity as separate compositions.

EXERCISE B

▶ Each of the following two paragraphs has problems with unity. First, identify the topic sentence or main idea of each paragraph. Then identify the problem sentences—that is, those sentences that do not *directly* relate to the topic sentence.

(1) Since the beginning of the season, our school baseball team has been amazing. Our school is amazing too because it has won the Provincial Championship for the past three years. Our team has won seven out of their last nine games, including a six-game consecutive winning streak, which ties the program record. Furthermore, our team has won six out of seven home games. They lost to the division champion in what everyone concedes was a very close game. The reason we lost that last game is that our best pitcher simply got tired. We used

Noel to start every single game, and in the last one he just got worn out. Now that our relief staff is stronger, we're an even better team. Next time around, we're bound to win the championship.

(2) My old house has lots of problems. Problems are sometimes difficult to handle; for instance, when people have marriage problems, they need to go to counsellors for help. In my house, the doors won't close properly. Sometimes, in fact, they stick, and we have to force them open. Another problem this old house has is its water pipes. They're really old and worn. If you are washing clothes, you can't take a shower. There simply is no water pressure. In fact, if any water is run, it will interrupt your shower. The roof also has some serious problems. It's a beautiful, old wood roof, but it is so worn that each rainstorm means more leaks. I think it will cost a fortune to fix my old house. And that's a problem, too!

Topic Sentences

If you can understand the purposes of a **topic sentence,** your writing will significantly improve. Determining unity becomes a relatively easy task once you are able to identify the topic sentence. You can think about the topic sentence as the seed out of which everything else grows. Or, you can think of it as the picture frame that brings order and meaning to your ideas. It helps your reader (and yourself) understand what you're trying to say and makes sense of your ideas. Look at the following example of a paragraph *without* a topic sentence:

> These games have been held in conjunction with the Olympics since 1976. The athletes compete in a variety of sports, including sledge hockey in the Winter Paralympics. There are six different disability groups, but the emphasis is on the athletic achievements rather than any disability. Canadian wheelchair sprinter Chantal Petitclerc dominated the Athens 2004 championships winning five gold medals. These elite athletes keep the ideals of sport and sportsmanship alive for us all.

Although you can "sense" what this paragraph is about, its meaning is *implicit,* that is, *understood in its context, but not directly stated.* Good academic writing makes meaning *explicit,* that is, *clearly stated* and this is the work of the topic sentence. Consider how much clearer the paragraph reads when we insert the following idea: "The Paralympics are elite sports competitions for athletes from all over the world." This topic sentence helps make sense of the paragraph that follows and gives you, the reader, that "aha!" experience of saying to yourself, "Oh, that's what it's all about."

The job of the topic sentence is to help make meaning explicit, clearer for the reader so he or she doesn't have to make guesses or even work too hard to figure out what he or she is reading. Experienced writers can place topic sentences in the middle or end of paragraphs, but it is better for newer writers to begin their paragraphs with the topic sentence. Your professors also expect to see paragraphs organized this way. Your textbooks generally are organized in this orderly way as well. All you need to do as you study is check off the topic sentences to know what ideas are to follow. This same experience—expectation and its fulfillment—is the basis of all strong academic writing.

However, fulfilling the expectations created by your topic sentence can be tricky. If you don't provide your reader with what is expected, your writing will not be focused and will lack unity. You can remedy much of these difficulties by identifying the **key words or controlling idea** of a topic sentence. Not only does this identification help check for paragraph unity, but it also helps in the actual writing of your paragraph.

Let's look at a few examples. In the following topic sentence, ask yourself what particular words identify the sentence's main idea:

Network television has become increasingly R-rated.

What is this sentence about? Clearly, *network television* and *R-rated* are the key words and controlling idea of this sentence. You can probably begin to fill in the examples that might illustrate this idea. We expect this paragraph *to show us how* network television has been changing. Every example needs to relate to this idea. The expectation is what the sentence is promising, committing itself to discuss.

Consider the following sentence. What are its key words and controlling idea? What do we expect to be reading about?

The economic boom of the 1990s was the most remarkable in our nation's history.

The key words for this sentence are *economic boom of the 1990s* and *most remarkable;* we expect to read about *why* the 1990s boom was the most remarkable. Here is the controlling idea; again, you might be able to provide examples and reasons to illustrate this idea. You might consider the way the new dot-com companies and the digital revolution contributed to this period's economic expansion. This paragraph, as the earlier one, will almost write itself—once you have identified the key words and controlling idea.

EXERCISE C

▶ Identify the key words and controlling idea for the following sentences. Be able to state the "expectation" of the sentence—what does the paragraph to follow need to show?

1. Hockey continues to be Canada's favourite sport.
2. Michaëlle Jean has significantly changed our view of the Governor General.
3. Eating a vegetarian diet will make you a healthier person.

Limit Your Topic Sentence by Asking Questions

One way to identify key words and controlling ideas in topic sentences is to ask the journalist's questions of *who? what? when? why? where?* and *how?* Quite often we find it hard to write because our main idea is unclear, too vague, or too general. Asking these questions will also help you refine and narrow your ideas.

The following topic sentence is far too *general:* "Celebrities make lots of money." If an idea is too general, it covers a large category. This sentence about "celebrities" could, for example, refer to celebrities in film or music (rock, rap, classical, jazz) or television or sports or art or politics. The category "celebrities" is too big. You might need as much as an entire essay—not a paragraph—to support this idea. Asking the question "Who?" would help narrow this very broad statement and make it more interesting too. Here are two possible revisions: "Rock groups like Nickelback make huge amounts of money" or "Wayne Gretzky has made a lot of money because of his celebrity." We now have a topic that is more *specific;* it is limited and precise. The next question you might ask is, "What do you mean by 'huge amounts of money' and 'a lot of money'?" The paragraph about the rock groups would provide specific examples and data about CD and concert sales to show the reader how much money these performers have made; similarly, the paragraph about Wayne Gretzky might list examples showing how his NHL playing, team ownership, and endorsements have made him a rich man. These two paragraphs would almost write themselves.

Being able to know as precisely as possible what it is you are trying to say will create good writing *and* make the writing itself go more smoothly.

EXERCISE D

▶ The following topic sentences need refining; they are too broad. Using the "journalist's questions," rewrite each sentence to add specific information that narrows the topic. Be prepared to explain which question you used in your revision and what other questions you might ask to explain or illustrate your controlling idea.

1. Different sports interest different people.

2. There are many good teachers at this school.

3. I like many television shows.

4. Poverty is a terrible social ill.

5. Fad diets usually don't work.

Coherence

The second principle of good paragraph (and essay) writing—**coherence**—goes hand in glove with the principle of unity. Coherence means two things: (1) to cohere or stick together and (2) to make sense logically. The opposite of coherence, then, means things have no order, make no sense, or fly off in every direction.

Certainly, having unity will remedy some coherence problems. However, even if all your sentences directly relate to your main idea, your paragraph may still be incoherent because it lacks logical relationships between its ideas. Coherence means that your paragraph has a clear structure and logical connections. As you read the paragraph below, ask yourself why it seems confused:

> Madonna's early costumes had her wearing what looked like underwear, bras, and slips. Sometimes these were worn over her clothing, sometimes all by themselves. Today, fashions for young women commonly include skirts and tops that could be undergarments. Because of changes in the way female pop performers dress, young women have been given permission to break the boundaries of what once was considered good taste. A fashion signature of singer Britney Spears is her tight clothing and bare midriff. Young girls—sometimes as young as nine years old—wear tight-fitting clothes and bare their midriffs. Fashion for young women and girls has certainly changed since the days when even a miniskirt was considered pushing the limits of taste and propriety.

This paragraph could work very well. It has general statements that provide context for its examples and a concluding closing sentence—all the components of a solid paragraph. But it is confused and incoherent; the paragraph doesn't progress logically, and its parts do not seem to "stick together" and work as a unit. Creating coherency means applying two principles: (1) providing a structural order and strategy controlling the development of the ideas and (2) providing transitions between the ideas that create a sense of "flow" from one sentence to the next.

Let's apply these two principles to the paragraph above. First, the paragraph plunges us immediately into an example. We are disoriented because we have no idea what the example about Madonna means. *Details without a topic sentence that acts as a controlling statement are confusing.* The main idea of the paragraph, its topic sentence, occurs in the fourth sentence: "Because of changes in the way female pop performers dress, young women have been given permission to break the boundaries of what once was considered good taste." Beginning the paragraph with this idea provides a context for the rest of the sentences—like suddenly being given a pair of glasses that allows us to see meaning and order—almost. Even with the topic sentence providing a logical context for the paragraph, it still has problems:

> Because of changes in the way female pop performers dress, young women have been given permission to break the boundaries of what once was considered good taste. Madonna's early costumes had her wearing what looked like underwear, bras, and slips. Sometimes these were worn over her clothing, sometimes all by themselves. Today, fashions for young women commonly include skirts and tops that could be undergarments. A fashion signature of singer Britney Spears is her tight clothing and bare midriff. Young girls—sometimes as young as nine years old—wear tight-fitting clothes and bare their midriffs. Fashion for young women and girls has certainly changed since the days when even a miniskirt was considered pushing the limits of taste and propriety.

After the topic sentence, the reader still has examples thrown at her or him without any preparation. Structurally, the paragraph uses the example of Madonna and Britney Spears to develop its main idea that female pop performers have radically changed fashion for young women. But we need sentences to prepare us for these examples as well as **transitions** or "bridges" between these ideas to help us see the ways they *explicitly* connect.

With only a few changes, we can significantly improve this paragraph. First, we can add two sentences that introduce Madonna and Britney Spears to the reader as examples of pop performers whose fashion sense has changed styles: "Madonna was one of the first pop performers whose clothing taste influenced the fashion scene" and "Britney Spears has also had a powerful influence on the way young women dress." These two sentences provide a bridge to each example and create a sense of logical transition.

We can also signal to the reader that the last sentence is a concluding thought by inserting the evaluative term "clearly." The paragraph now reads smoothly and easily:

> Because of changes in the way female pop performers dress, young women have been given permission to break the boundaries of what once was considered good taste. Madonna was one of the first pop performers whose clothing taste influenced the fashion scene. Madonna's early costumes had her wearing what looked like underwear, bras, and slips. Sometimes these were worn over her clothing, sometimes all by themselves. Today, fashions for young women commonly include skirts and tops that could be undergarments. Britney Spears has also had a powerful influence on the way young women dress. A fashion signature of singer Britney Spears is her tight clothing and bare midriff. Young girls—sometimes as young as nine years old—wear tight-fitting clothes and bare their midriffs. Clearly, fashion for young women and girls has certainly changed since the days when even a miniskirt was considered pushing the limits of taste and propriety.

Notice that several key phrases from the topic sentence are repeated at transition points: "Madonna was one of the first *pop performers* whose clothing taste influenced the fashion scene" and "Britney Spears has also had a powerful influence on the way *young women dress*." The *repetition of key words and phrases* will create a sense of structure and order in your writing.

This exercise teaches us two other very important lessons. First, we can see how important it is to **have a clear topic sentence, a controlling statement.** Second, by **inserting either framing sentences or "transition" signal words,** we can quickly remedy problems of coherency. Making order sometimes is as simple as adding a word or two or three. In the sentences right above, "first" and "second" are transition words that create a relationship between the sentences and, hence, a sense of order.

Common Transition Words and Phrases

Consequence
> therefore, then, thus, hence, accordingly, as a result

Adding Information
> also, again, in addition, too

Likeness and Example

> likewise, similarly, for instance, for example

Contrast

> but, however, yet, on the contrary

Sequence, Time Order

> first, second, third, next, finally

Restatement

> in other words, that is

Conclusion

> in conclusion, finally, therefore, thus

Concession

> of course, it is true

By simply inserting sequence words or phrases such as "for example," you can instantly create coherence *and* give your writing the feel of sophisticated academic writing.

EXERCISE E

▶ Create order in the following paragraph by using the transition words and phrases listed above. You do not need to add any more sentences.

> Everyone needs food. You'd think we'd know how to eat properly to maintain our health and well-being. Too many Canadians are eating the wrong way and the wrong food, as a nation we are becoming fat and unhealthy. Over half of Canadians are overweight, and heart disease and Type 2 diabetes are contributing to billions of dollars in health care costs. Too many people, young and old, are getting fat from inactivity. They are sitting in front of televisions or computers, or driving a car instead of getting exercise. We're eating too much and too often, substituting the empty calories of sugary snacks for nutritious foods. Canada has a food guide and a variety of government departments to handle food regulations. We lack solid policies to shift consumers to healthier choices. The 2006 decision to introduce mandatory nutrition labelling of trans-fats for most packaged goods will go a long way to encourage manufacturers to reduce the amounts of these harmful fats and to help Canadians make better food choices.

Organizing Your Ideas: Structures and Strategies

Smooth transitions between sentences certainly help create order and coherence in writing. But smooth transitions cannot occur without a clear structure controlling how we arrange our ideas. Good writers are aware of ordering strategies or appropriate idea frameworks. There are many different ways to structure your writing strategically. We will look at two dominant patterns and then at four developmental strategies.

Deductive and Inductive Patterns: A Matter of Effect

At a basic level, who we are—our particular temperaments—has a lot to do with what organizing structures we choose. Some of us are detail-oriented people, and some of us come up with generalizations at the drop of a hat. Generally speaking, people for whom generalizations are easy will tend to gravitate to a **deductive development;** people who find they can easily write details will gravitate to an **inductive development.** Understanding your "writing temperament" as well as the way these two large developmental patterns work will help you be a more masterful writer.

Deductive Development: From General to Specific

We are all most familiar with deductive development, for in this structure we begin with a general idea—a topic sentence—and then use specifics in the rest of the paragraph to develop it, explain it, illustrate it, or defend it.

All the examples in this book use deductive development. Starting your paragraph with a good topic sentence (which is, as you know, a general statement of what your paragraph is about) helps the reader know what to expect.

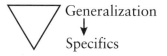
Generalization
↓
Specifics

This is the format used most in business and academic writing because it is the easiest to read. The following paragraph is a good example of **deductive development;** the topic sentence is in italics:

> The federal government [also] took measures to combat widespread anti-immigrant attitudes during the war. *Ironically, while attempting to unite Canadians, the government meted out harsh treatment to members of ethnic groups whose homelands were at war with Canada, believing that they constituted a danger to the state.* Under the War Measures Act, the federal government interned hundreds of German Canadians, although the RCMP found no evidence of domestic subversion. Upon Italy's entry into the war, the RCMP began to fingerprint and photograph thousands of Italian Canadians, and arrested some 700. Businessman James Franceschini was one of those interned; he saw his business placed in the hands of the Custodian of Alien Property and the equipment sold off at fire-sale prices to his Montreal competitors. A few members of the clergy and university professors questioned the arrests. Most Canadians appeared, by their silence, to acquiesce.
>
> from *Journeys: A History of Canada*

The topic sentence clearly asserts its position: "… the government meted out harsh treatment to members of ethnic groups whose homelands were at war with Canada," and we expect that the paragraph will show us in what way this statement is accurate—that is, if the paragraph performs its task well. Certainly, there are enough examples to affirm its assertion, and we accept that, yes, the government was harsh in its treatment of those ethnic groups from countries with whom Canada was then at war. This structure of a generalization supported by specifics has no difficulty communicating its meaning—a good reason why it is the preferred pattern in business and education. But it is not the only way to organize ideas.

Inductive Development: From Specific to General

Another pattern inverts deductive development so that it moves from specifics to a generalization or **inductive development.** Inductive development actually replicates the way most people think. Many of us gather information, details, and data from which we infer a generalization. Scientific method uses this type of reasoning—as do detectives in mystery stories. Consider how often Sherlock Holmes puts pieces of information together to find out the truth so that at the end of the story he can utter, "Elementary, my dear Watson." This way of organizing ideas is certainly legitimate, but notice the effect it has on your ease of comprehension in the following paragraph; the topic sentence, again, is in italics:

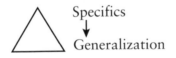

     With Whitaker's facts and the facts of the subscription lists before us, we seem to have arrived at three facts which are indisputable and must have great influence upon our enquiry how we can help you to prevent war. The first is that the daughters of educated men are paid very little from the public funds for their public service; the second is that they are paid nothing at all from the public funds for their private services; and the third is that their share of the husband's income is not a flesh-and-blood share but a spiritual or nominal share, which means that when both are clothed and fed, the surplus funds that can be devoted to causes, pleasures or philanthropies gravitate mysteriously but indisputably toward those causes, pleasures and philanthropies which the husband enjoys, and of which the husband approves. *It seems that the person to whom the salary is actually paid is the person who has the actual right to decide how that salary shall be spent.*

Virginia Woolf, Three Guineas

If you found this paragraph a little hard to follow, you're not alone. Once you read the last sentence, the topic sentence, the paragraph starts to make some sense; if you reread the paragraph starting with the topic sentence, then its meaning becomes substantially clearer. This paragraph, by the great British novelist and essayist Virginia Woolf, isn't confusing because of its length (it is long) but because of its organization. It keeps you in suspense until its final sentence—the generalization that provides the controlling idea for the paragraph. The purpose of this kind of organization is to keep you in suspense, to keep you wondering, caught in the magic of fine language, until that final thought. However, you can see why it is a questionable pattern for situations that demand immediate clarity—as in tests, school papers, and business communication. So you can use this pattern, but be aware of its effect and use it accordingly.

This pattern, as noted above, also replicates the way many people think. You may find that you write your first drafts using inductive development. If that proves true, you can easily restructure your paragraphs by simply moving your final general idea to the beginning of the paragraph. If you are uncertain whether your paragraph has a general idea or topic sentence, check to see if it emerges at the end of your paragraphs. Although we aren't discussing essays here, the same principle applies in essay writing. Many times we "discover" our thesis or essay's purpose in our conclusion. If you are an inductive thinker, look for your main ideas in your final, concluding thoughts.

EXERCISE A

▶ Determine whether the following paragraphs use *inductive* or *deductive* patterns of development. Be sure you underline the topic sentence of each paragraph.

1. I am convinced that there is no place to live that is free from the threat of water. For five years I lived on a beach at less than two metres above sea level. Each time there was a hurricane at sea, I had to board up the house and evacuate to higher ground. Finally exhausted from the years of facing the danger of flooding, I moved to an inland province. Because my new home was 150 metres above sea level, I felt safe. But I had lived there only two weeks when a creek that was barely visible from my house overflowed and sent water flooding my downstairs. As I watched the muddy water keep rising over the lower level of my home, I wondered what safe spot I could move to next—perhaps Saskatchewan.

Deductive _____ *Inductive* _____

2. In October [1956], despite strong American opposition, Israel, together with Britain and France, invaded Egypt, in response to Egypt's nationalization of the Suez Canal. Wary of the dangerous split developing in the western alliance, [Canada's Prime Minister Lester B.] Pearson proposed the creation of a multinational United Nations emergency peacekeeping force in the region. For his efforts, he won the Nobel Peace Prize in 1957. According to biographer John English, Pearson's initiative "strengthened the United Nations, moderated the tensions between Washington and London, and helped to maintain both the Commonwealth and NATO."

from Journeys: A History of Canada

Deductive _____ *Inductive* _____

3. Rainforests contain nearly half of all the plants and animals in the world—many of which have unique medical properties that humans must save from extinction. Some rainforest plants are used to treat Hodgkin's disease, multiple sclerosis, and Parkinson's disease. A delicate, tiny blue periwinkle flower found only in Madagascar, for example, is the key element in a drug used to treat leukemia. Ecologist Norman Myers estimates there are five million rainforest species found nowhere else in the world, and many are becoming extinct before we ever discover what wonder drugs they contain.

Sally Lujetic

Deductive _____ *Inductive* _____

4. **Now write your own paragraph:** First use *inductive structure*; after you have your inductive paragraph, make the appropriate revisions so that you re-create it in *deductive structure*. Here are some possible topic areas:

Your favourite rock performer   *Your dream job*
Your favourite television show   *The holiday you like least*

After you write your paragraphs, be ready to discuss how the different organizing patterns influence the communication of your ideas.

Structural Strategies: The Top Four

Whether you use a deductive or inductive pattern, your paragraph will need further structural organizing. Masterful writing is writing in which ideas have been artfully ordered. No matter how brilliant your ideas may be, if they are presented in an incoherent manner, their brilliance will be lost. Therefore, being conscious of effective organizing strategies will significantly improve your writing. Although there are many strategic ways to arrange your ideas, we're going to concentrate on what we believe are the top four formats—formats that are also most common in the academic and business arenas.

Order of Importance: A Matter of Intention

A fundamental strategy in organizing your ideas is to rank them in terms of their **order of importance.** You can order ideas from *least to most important* or from *most to least important.* Both your audience and your intention—the purpose of your writing—will determine which order you choose. For example, in business, where time is of the essence and people work under a lot of pressure, written communication needs to get to the point immediately. Therefore, ideas tend to be organized *most to least important.* The reader, the intended audience, may not even read to the end of the document. This format has also been true for traditional journalism, another area in which the reader wants information quickly. More literary, argumentative, and persuasive writing, however, may want to hold the reader to the very end of the written piece. This kind of writing not only informs but also may try to influence the writer's views. In this context, using the format of least to most important makes the most sense.

Consider these two paragraphs, which have the same information, just different formats:

Most to Least Important

> Over a million children living in one of the world's richest countries, Canada, are living below the poverty line. In 1989 Canada resolved to eliminate child poverty by 2000, but fifteen years later the percentage of poor children had actually increased. This means that for the one in six Canadian children who are living in poverty, the stresses on their families may put them in danger of abuse or neglect. These children may not see a doctor or dentist regularly. Too many may not be properly nourished, or may live in substandard housing. Children who live in poverty can even be forced into emergency shelter when their parents fall behind in the rent. Furthermore, they miss out on the enrichment opportunities that middle-class children take for granted: family vacations, music lessons, participation in community sports teams, a home computer for schoolwork. They can't buy the "in" clothing or accessories like MP3 players that help a student adjust socially. They fall behind in school, and they are unlikely to catch up.

Least to Most Important

Over a million children in one of the world's richest countries, Canada, are living in poverty. Fifteen years after the Canadian Government unanimously resolved to eliminate child poverty by the year 2000, the rate had actually increased to nearly one in six children. These are the children who will fall behind and may never catch up. They lack the social accessories of middle-class children, like the "in" clothing and MP3 players. They don't have the enrichment opportunities of better-off children, like family vacations, music lessons, or participation in extracurricular sports teams. They fall behind for many reasons; one simply that they have no home computer. They are less healthy because their families struggle to buy nourishing food. In fact, 40 percent of food bank users are children, although they only make up 26 percent of the population. Poor children are less likely to see a doctor, and rarely see a dentist. They often live in substandard housing, and some are forced into emergency shelter when their parents fall behind in the rent. The stresses of poverty on the family can lead to neglect or even abuse of the children. And this is happening among people who are working, in a society that says it values work and children.

We have enlarged the second paragraph to emphasize the argumentative effect of using the least to most important format. Both formats work to inform; the second paragraph consciously wants to hold your attention to make its point felt strongly.

Organizing by Examples

If you want a strong paragraph—or any writing to be strong and effective—be sure you supply specifics for those general statements that make up your framework. In fact, the more vivid details a paragraph has, the stronger and more interesting it will be. A principle of good writing is "Show; don't tell!" The most common way we "show" is to supply specifics to our writing through examples. In the paragraph below, the topic sentence, *Their fear led them to develop elaborate rituals to ward off encounters with the dead*, is made vivid and meaningful for us through the use of three very interesting examples:

Once people were very much afraid of ghosts. *Their fear led them to develop elaborate rituals to ward off encounters with the dead*. For example, because primitive people believed that ghosts could capture their spirits at funerals, they carried wooden images of themselves in hopes that the ghosts would be fooled into carrying off the images. It is possible, too, that the tradition of sitting up with the dead comes from a belief that ghosts escape in the night. Certainly the ritual of laying tombstones is derived from a superstition about the dead. People once believed that stones piled on top of a grave would keep the dead person's ghost from escaping and haunting the living. Eventually the number of stones diminished until only one stone, the tombstone, was left as a reminder of the ancient superstition.

This paragraph develops deductively (the topic sentence/generalization is at the beginning) and uses the least to most important order to present its examples. The final example about tombstones is the most interesting and is given the most weight by having the most discussion. This paragraph illustrated its main idea by using several examples, but you can also use one extended example to make your point:

> *If the coach of our baseball team doesn't learn to get along with us, our team may not stay together.* Last night, for example, we played against a team we should have beaten. However, the coach created a terribly tense environment. He kept picking on Darryl, one of our best hitters. When Darryl struck out, the coach exploded in anger, chewed him out, and threatened to bench him. Darryl was shaken, and so were the rest of us. When Darryl tried to defend himself, the coach just yelled at him to "Shut up and get out of my way!" We were all so upset that we couldn't play at our best. We lost.

This example—actually an anecdote—vividly shows us how the coach's behaviour may result in destroying the team. Whether you use extended examples like this one or interesting facts as in the earlier paragraph, using examples helps your reader understand your idea and makes for a satisfying reading experience.

Organizing by Classification

Another common way of organizing ideas is to use classification. We use classification all the time in our daily lives. For example, consider how you might arrange your clothing. First, you might set up a category for winter and summer clothing. Then within these two classes, you could have a place for sweaters, pants, suits, shirts, and shoes for your winter clothes and tops, shorts, swimsuits, and sandals for your summer clothes. You probably also create categories or classifications for your music. For instance, you might have a classical section, a blues section, and a rock section. This same method applies to writing. In this method, you arrange your details into categories that you then present in your paragraph. The following paragraph is a good example:

> There are three particularly unpleasant types of roommates. I have lived in a college dormitory for four years, and I have experienced all three. Perhaps the least offensive is the poor-housekeeper type. I roomed with one during my freshman year. When I returned from my first day of classes, I discovered that while I was away from the room, it had positively snowed papers and clothes. In my second year, I traded the messy roommate for a bossy one. This roommate was an expert in every field; she knew just how to arrange furniture, fold clothes, sharpen pencils, and study for exams. And she never let me suffer a moment for want of her advice. Still, even the bossy type of roommate can be endured more easily than the third type—the confirmed borrower. This roommate never had a pen, an English book, or a change of clothes. But she did not mind; I had a ready supply of all three. Of course, I could never count on being able to write a history paper, study my English assignment, or dress for a special date, but my roommate could. I have lived with all three types of unpleasant roommates, and I will settle for the messy type any day.

This is a classic academic paragraph. Its organizational strategies have a lot to teach us. First, it is a fine example of organizing by using classification. The writer has sorted her roommate experiences into three categories: messy, bossy, and borrower. Second, it uses examples as well. Notice how she offers examples of what each roommate type means. Not only do we get a vivid sense of each type, but we also understand what the writer means because your idea of messy may be quite different from hers. The writer also has chosen to present her details using the least to most order—this time, least obnoxious to most obnoxious. Last, the writer arranges her information chronologically, beginning with her first year in college through her senior year. The effect of these ordering frames is to create a very coherent and readable piece of writing. It provides an excellent model for your own paragraphs.

Organizing by Comparison and Contrast

Comparison and contrast is another very common, often used strategy to organize ideas. We compare and contrast frequently in our daily lives, too. You may choose one restaurant over another because you have silently compared and contrasted them: This one has better steaks, that one better chicken; this one has finer wine, that one a better selection of beer. Or you may compare and contrast when buying clothes: This blouse is my favourite colour, but that one has pretty buttons; this blouse is cheap, but that blouse fits better.

Although we use this way of thinking a great deal, compare/contrast organizing strategies have special demands. First, you need to compare and contrast for a **purpose.** Just comparing two things at random is meaningless. *The reason you compare and contrast is your topic sentence!* Second, comparisons also necessitate thinking in terms of **categories.** In the previous paragraph, we just implicitly created two categories for restaurant food evaluation: main courses and drinks. Last, comparison/contrast organizing strategies **demand balance:** What you say about one item needs to be said about the other. You go back and forth— it's like playing ping-pong, but with ideas. Let's look at an example:

> *Movie directors are able to make use of several techniques not available to directors of live theatre.* First, **in film** flashbacks are very easily handled without cumbersome changes of scenes. *In contrast,* **in live theatre** these can sometimes be distracting. Second, **in film** it is easy to get inside the minds of the actors, to hear their unspoken thoughts. The camera just zooms in for a close-up, and the audience hears their words, but their lips don't move. *However,* **in live theatre** the actor usually looks directly at the audience and speaks these lines. The audience may sometimes confuse these private thoughts with the other dialogue of the play. Finally, **movies** can have an extravagant array of settings. It is easy to film almost any setting—mountains, beaches, or the inside of buildings—and use those sequences as backdrops for the action. **Live theatre,** *on the contrary, requires elaborate, hand-painted scenes. These are often very heavy and must be moved about several times during the performance. Movie directors thus have* greater flexibility than live theatre can offer in the uses of flashbacks, unspoken thoughts, and setting.

First, the point of this comparison and contrast is clearly stated in the topic sentences: "Movie directors are able to make use of several techniques not available to directors of live theatre." Second, the paragraph is organized around three categories: flashbacks, unspoken thoughts, and setting. Third, the paragraph plays ping-pong—it jumps back and forth between film and live theatre. *There is a balance between the two discussions.* Balance is critical to good compare-and-contrast writing. What you say about one thing, you must say about the other. Notice the transition words (in italics) that indicate contrast. They not only move the ideas along but also make explicit the paragraph's intention.

Because **balance** is so important to this organizing strategy, it helps to learn the two patterns that create models for comparison and contrast writing. The paragraph above plays literary ping-pong—jumps back and forth between the two things being discussed. This model looks like this:

  I. Category (Flashbacks)

    A. (Film)
    B. (Live Theatre)

  II. Category (Unspoken Thoughts)

    A. (Film)
    B. (Live Theatre)

  III. Category (Setting)

    A. (Film)
    B. (Live Theatre)

There is another model for writing comparison and contrast; rather than playing ping-pong, it divides the essay in half, first discussing one item in relation to the categories and then discussing the other—again in relation to the same categories. (Remember: Balance is key to this form of writing.) This model looks like this:

  I. Item (Film)

    A. Category (Flashbacks)
    B. Category (Unspoken Thoughts)
    C. Category (Setting)

  II. Item (Live Theatre)

    A. Category (Flashbacks)
    B. Category (Unspoken Thoughts)
    C. Category (Setting)

Because you are dividing your discussion in half, a problem with this second method can occur if you forget to continue the same categories or get so tired out that you short-change the second item in your discussion.

EXERCISE B

▶ The best way to learn to write is to write! Modelling is an excellent way to learn. In the following exercises, we will ask you to model your own paragraphs after the ones used in the discussion above.

1. Rewrite the paragraph about film and live theatre using the second model.

2. Write your own comparison/contrast paragraph. First you'll need to come up with a topic area. Here are some ideas: two contrasting or similar performers, two cars, two sport-utility vehicles, two TV shows that are similar (for example, two situation comedies or hospital or police shows). Outline your paragraph.

3. Using the classification paragraph on roommates as a model, write your own classification paragraph.

4. Write a paragraph that uses one extended example to illustrate its topic sentence.

TROUBLESHOOTING: REVISION

Once you have written a draft of your paragraph, the next step is to revise it, to look at it as a whole for unity and coherence. Remember: All good writing is rewriting. Read your work out loud. Listen for any problems, rough areas, moments when you pause, when the reading is confusing. These areas probably have some mechanical errors. Paragraphs offer up their own unique difficulties. Here are some checklists to help you refine your final drafts.

1. If your writing sounds confused or unclear, check:

- Do you have a topic sentence?
- Do you have an organizational strategy?
- Do you have transitions between sentences?

2. Is your paragraph too vague and general?

- Be sure you have enough examples, details, and specifics to explain or illustrate the main idea thoroughly.

3. Do you have too many details with no explicit reason for them?

- Be sure you have a topic sentence by underlining the topic sentence and checking that each sentence is on topic.

4. Is your paragraph too long?

- Remember how important *white space* is. We need to rest our eyes. If your paragraph runs a page or more, break it up into smaller paragraphs. A decent paragraph is about seven to eleven lines long.

5. Is your paragraph too short?

- Too short a paragraph may be a red flag. Academic writing explains, shows, and illustrates ideas, which usually takes several sentences.
- If you tend to write very short paragraphs, check for the following possible problems:

    a. Do your paragraphs need to be developed further? Do you have enough specifics?

    b. Do your short paragraphs need to be combined together into one under a topic sentence?

- If all the ideas relate directly to the same general notion, then you may need to create a topic sentence and combine the paragraphs under it, or use the topic sentence you have and combine the other paragraphs.
- Again, *generally*, academic paragraphs are about seven to eleven lines long. *But this is not a rule.* Paragraphs can be of any length. You need to be able to decide whether or not you have adequately explained your ideas.

TROUBLESHOOTING: EDITING

Once you have revised your draft to make it a more unified, coherent, and well-organized piece of writing, you are ready to "fine-tune" the sentences by careful editing. **Editing** is checking each sentence for good grammar and usage, reviewing all the basics you have been working with throughout this text. Once you have identified errors, reviewing the rules will help you make corrections.

1. Read the passage "backwards," from last sentence to first. (But read each sentence in its normal order.) This will help you find any *run-ons* or *sentence fragments* (Chapters 11, 12).

2. Read your writing aloud to check for *punctuation* that makes meaning clear (Units 3, 4), *parallel structure* (Chapter 24), and *dangling modifiers* (Chapter 23).

3. Circle the verbs to help you check for *verb tense consistency* and *subject–verb agreement* (Chapter 5).

4. Check that *pronouns* are in the right form (Chapters 17, 18) and that they agree with their antecedents, the words for which they substitute (Chapter 19).

When you are able to identify these problem areas in your writing, and make the necessary corrections through revision and editing, you will be well equipped for academic success, and you will become a better communicator.

Answers to "A" Exercises

Exercise 1A

1. Chocolate is
2. It comes
3. people call
4. Europeans tasted
5. conquerors found
6. Aztecs crushed
7. Hernan Cortez brought
8. Spaniards used
9. chocolate spread
10. drinking was
11. public gathered
12. reputation was
13. Chocolate existed
14. candy appeared
15. name is
16. Laura Secord was
17. Laura Secord trekked
18. chocolate maker named
19. Canadian purchases
20. Eating has
21. chocolate contains
22. substance seems
23. components improve
24. They act

Exercise 2A

1. people know / name is
2. townships have / California named
3. Meteorologists mention
4. current flows influences
5. Humboldt made helped

6. people describe / writers call
7. he went
8. He observed wrote
9. companion was
10. Humboldt Bonpland had
11. They travelled climbed
12. situation was / they carried
13. They used / they climbed
14. hands were / he stopped
15. exploits attracted
16. Jefferson admired / men enjoyed
17. Humboldt reviewed published
18. interests included / Humboldt gave

Exercise 3A

1. I discovered
2. name is
3. dog exists / origin dates
4. ancestors came
5. tribes bred
6. Centuries produced
7. tribes used
8. dogs became were
9. preservation is
10. LaFlamme used
11. purpose was
12. dogs resemble / they are
13. colour ranges
14. It is
15. owners give
16. Names include
17. Preserving gives
18. It provides
19. you want / information is

Exercise 4A

1. you Have heard
2. Jindo is protected / it has been designated
3. dog has had
4. Jindo is named
5. island was separated
6. breed was recognized
7. Korea was occupied / professor became
8. professor was impressed
9. intelligence can be / dogs are
10. Jindos will listen / they will obey
11. They can outsmart will try
12. Jindos are attached / people have found
13. Jindos have been known
14. owners move / Jindos travel
15. Jindos were brought
16. Jindos were meant / people have bred
17. breeds are used
18. Jindo remains / owner can tolerate

Exercise 5A

1. is
2. is
3. exist
4. are
5. were
6. comes
7. equals
8. are
9. is
10. is
11. focuses
12. opens
13. is

14. determines
15. is
16. Do / interest
17. serve
18. is
19. broadens

Exercise 6A

1. Does
2. is
3. require
4. goes
5. need
6. offers
7. is
8. Has
9. has
10. prefer
11. thinks
12. is
13. makes
14. is
15. adds
16. is
17. makes
18. saves
19. is
20. reflects
21. feature
22. enjoys
23. convince
24. goes

Exercise 7A

1. is
2. meets
3. goes

4. continues
5. is
6. are
7. plans
8. agrees
9. is
10. causes
11. stands
12. is
13. was
14. Is
15. looks
16. is
17. Have
18. is
19. meets
20. affects
21. is
22. comes
23. Has
24. visits

Exercise 8A

1. competes
2. decides
3. needs
4. contribute
5. were
6. has
7. Is
8. seems
9. is
10. Does
11. was
12. Is
13. are
14. are
15. comes

16. were
17. keeps
18. sit
19. needs
20. cost
21. comes
22. makes
23. has
24. improves

Exercise 9A

1. Peter Pan, for
2. 1904; however, few
3. C
4. him, and
5. best, so
6. fourteen; James
7. up; therefore, like
8. C
9. Ansell; however, the
10. children; thus, he
11. died; subsequently, Barrie
12. stories, and
13. C
14. Henley, and
15. Barrie; she
16. lisped; consequently, she
17. him, for
18. *Peter Pan;* nevertheless, her

Exercise 10A

1. Although most of us think there is only one Peter Pan story,
2. so that the sons of the Llewelyn Davies could perform in them. C

3. where he is introduced in one of the novel's episodes. C
4. <u>After the novel was published</u>,
5. <u>Because the play was so successful</u>,
6. <u>As if Barrie wanted to confuse us with all his Peter Pan versions</u>,
7. requirements, it
8. woman, and
9. 1915, but
10. actresses; they
11. systems, all
12. Peter Pans, some
13. Peter, and
14. 2003; it
15. C

Exercise 11A

Corrections will vary. The following are possible answers.

1. Because computers . . . another, it
2. at home, for this
3. number; however, they
4. C
5. If people . . . offices, the time
6. insurance, and
7. clothes because they
8. time, so they
9. time, nor do they have to work
10. home, and one of
11. coworkers, so they
12. promoted because their
13. true; therefore, working
14. distractions because employees
15. housework; however, telecommuters
16. Although working . . . money, there
17. office; in addition, they
18. advantages; nevertheless, it is

Exercise 12A

Corrections will vary. The following are possible answers.

1. 1937, the
2. equator, Earhart
3. death stated that
4. C
5. death exist because
6. research, a retired
7. theory connected
8. mission, for
9. Islands, Earhart
10. C
11. Bolam so that
12. work was based
13. 1965, Gervais
14. medallion resembling
15. photos from the 1930s in order
16. Earhart because
17. 1982, Bolam
18. She stated, however, that
19. cremated, and the
20. Earhart, she

Exercise 13A

1. are, I believe, in
2. and, therefore, deserve
3. For example, the
4. of us, however, are
5. are, in fact, also
6. C
7. Moreover, the
8. You, I'm sure, have
9. activities, for instance, farming

10. In addition, hunters
11. infant; therefore, this
12. animals; however, they
13. Consequently, many
14. again; however, adult
15. intelligent; in fact, they
16. For example, orangutans
17. intelligent, in fact, that
18. C
19. tragic, wouldn't it, if

Exercise 14A

1. you, like . . . Winkle, had
2. Age, a time . . . technology, had
3. television, a bulky . . . picture, was
4. display, a gel medium, or LCD, a liquid . . . display, for
5. once, "picture in picture," on
6. device, a lightweight headset, allowing
7. laptop, a small . . .
8. cellular phone, now
9. players, digital . . . devices, you
10. people, ten . . . teens, moving
11. device, an MP3, with
12. satellites, constantly orbiting, would
13. age, just . . . before, really
14. "office," a small . . . hand, is
15. C
16. teachers, remembering . . . times, ask . . . people, once . . . readers, now
17. devices, compact . . . inexpensive, are

Exercise 15A

1. (commercial,) which was an image of a Bulova watch face, was
2. (Ebbets Field,) where the Dodgers and Phillies were playing a baseball game.
3. (fee) that Bulova paid to broadcast this commercial, which was a remarkably low nine dollars, seems (Both clauses describe the word *fee*.)
4. (programs) that attract large numbers of viewers. C
5. (effects) that television commercials may have on our lives. C
6. (slogan) that appears in an especially memorable commercial may (ways) that have nothing to do with the original product. C
7. (slogan) . . . myself!," which appeared in commercials for the pain-killer Anacin, was
8. (Show,) which was one of the most popular variety shows of that era.
9. (slogan) that also achieved national fame appeared. C
10. (slogan,) which was "Where's the beef?," became . . . (proposals) that promised more than they could reasonably hope to deliver.
11. (products) that are being advertised. C
12. (venues) that include commercials made just for viewing on the Internet. C
13. (messages) that are known as "spam." C
14. (SPAM,) which is the name of a commercial meat product made by the Hormel Company.
15. (TiVo,) which enables viewers to delete commercials, and other
16. (consumers) who are willing to buy products, it C

Exercise 16A

NOTE: The comma before the final item in a series is optional.

1. London, England, in September, 1998, few
2. June 2, 1999, and *Harry*
3. June 8, 2000, the fourth . . . June 21, 2003.
4. April, 1995, Philip

5. *The Golden Compass, The Subtle Knife,* and *The Amber Spyglass.*
6. November 20, 2004, to April 2, 2005.
7. special effects, wonderful acting, and entertaining plot.
8. a setting in an imaginary world, a hero on a quest, and a battle
9. Sudbury, Ontario, to San Francisco, California.
10. December 26, 2007, through January 4, 2008.
11. Street, Suite 900, San Francisco, California
12. maps of the city, a list of places to visit, and even
13. English, Spanish, French, Italian, and Japanese.
14. Avenue, Daly City, California
15. C

Exercise 17A

1. I brought the papers to them.
2. He opened the door for her.
3. We gave you great advice.
4. I rode the subway with him . . .
5. They explained the project to me.
6. He invited us to the party.
7. me
8. We
9. he
10. she
11. us
12. me
13. him
14. I
15. we
16. She
17. me
18. he
19. us
20. us

Exercise 18A

1. I
2. her
3. I
4. themselves
5. they
6. me
7. my brother and me
8. He and I . . . than she
9. themselves
10. you and me
11. We pet lovers
12. than I
13. C
14. themselves
15. boyfriend plans (no *he*)
16. She and her boyfriend
17. C
18. you and me
19. C
20. than he

Exercise 19A

1. her
2. their
3. its
4. her
5. he or she (In this and similar answers, it would be equally correct to use only a masculine or only a feminine pronoun or to reword the sentence so that the antecedent and its pronouns become plural.)
6. his or her
7. C
8. he or she / his or her
9. his or her
10. his or her

11. Natasha and me
12. than I
13. you and me
14. We neighbours
15. My father always (no *he*) . . . brother and me
16. C
17. his or her birthday . . . he or she could have
18. he or she
19. John and me
20. We students

Exercise 20A

1. It's
2. Who's
3. their
4. My best friend and I
5. C
6. they're
7. It's . . . you're
8. whose . . . its
9. theirs
10. Yours
11. than they
12. friends and me
13. Julia and I / its prices
14. it's hers, not yours
15. They're . . . my family and I
16. C
17. We campers
18. Ours . . . its front
19. the person who's handling . . . the one whose skills
20. his or her

Exercise 21A

1. Canadian Automobile Association, Canada
2. Smalls, Ontario, Manitoba, Saskatchewan, Alberta, British Columbia, Pacific Rim National Park
3. July, August
4. Ontario, Lake Superior, Kenora, Lake of the Woods
5. Harvey Pentaman, Erickson, Manitoba
6. Manitoban, Neepawa, Margaret Laurence's, Manawaka, *A Jest of God, Rachel, Rachel,* Paul Newman, Joanne Woodward
7. Saskatchewan's, Royal Canadian Mounted Police, Regina
8. Banff, Jasper National Parks, Alberta, Columbia Icefields, Daniella, Stefan, Ian, Kevin, Drumheller, Alberta
9. The Dinosaur Capital of the World, UNESCO World Heritage Site, Royal Tyrell Museum
10. Tyrannosaurus Rex, Albertosaurus, *Jurassic Park*
11. Government of Alberta, Ministry of Community Development, September
12. Wades, Edmonton, West Edmonton Mall
13. Galaxyland Amusement Park, Sea Life Caverns, World Waterpark, Swiss Chalet, A&W, Harveys
14. Kelowna, Okanagan Lake, British Columbia, Stefan's, August
15. Vancouver's, Stanley Park, Capilano, Daniella, Under the Sea and Over the River, Communications, University of Western Ontario
16. Victoria, Vancouver Island, Smalls
17. Clayoquot Sound, Pacific Rim National Park
18. Western Canada, Unionville, Ontario, When

Exercise 22A

Part 1

1. time—but just barely—late
2. active: volunteering
3. said, "Ask . . . country"?
4. "Sonnet 18," the speaker asks, "Shall . . . day?"
5. professors'
6. soft, gentle
7. C

8. Dickens' [or Dickens's] novel *Hard Times* / "Coketown."
9. fields: computer
10. Sylvia's . . . promotion—a complete surprise to her—comes
11. "When . . . book," the professor said, "be . . . cover."
12. men's / women's
13. Olympics, the bobsledders

Part 2
Paragraph 1

exclaimed, "Slow down!"
By . . . quickly, I
car's back seat
brother's face
choices: to stop
"Young Adults and the Perils of Driving," but
anyone's

Paragraph 2

Toronto Star's lead
"Too Young to Drive?"
driver's chances
factors: lack
Still . . . yesterday's . . . mishap, I
paper's editorial
careful, competent
driver—teenager

Exercise 23A

Answers will vary. The following are possible revisions.

1. After she cleaned the floor, the mop
2. The lonely woman with a shuffling gait walked
3. C
4. bride dressed in ivory silk chiffon looked
5. With a loud voice, the professor
6. After the heroine married the prince,
7. The man eating the most hot dogs won

8. While I was driving . . . summer, my car's
9. a present wrapped in pink and blue paper to
10. C
11–15. Answers will vary.

Exercise 24A

Answers will vary. The following are possible revisions.

1. to cook, to read . . . , and to travel
2. mastered not only the guitar but also
3. is going either to
4. C
5. bought both a new
6. to study hard, to choose . . . and to phone home
7. energy, and enthusiasm
8. angry, and pessimistic
9. lines not only in the studio but also
10. Living on your own
11. and to have a substitute
12. want you neither to stop studying nor to stop
13. C
14. and too expensive
15. to manage not only their money but also their time

Exercise 25A

1. stuck
2. ridden
3. fell
4. understood
5. threw
6. set
7. rung
8. knew
9. read
10. hurt

11. met
12. swam
13. felt
14. drove
15. caught
16. laid
17. swore
18. lay
19. taken
20. chose
21. grown
22. rose
23. paid
24. fed
25. sank
26. won
27. written
28. stolen
29. kept
30. flew

Exercise 26A

Paragraph 1

My new car has made me very happy. . . . I simply love my new car.

Paragraph 2

My job makes me crazy. . . . My job is straining my sanity.

Exercise 27A

1. Deductive
2. Inductive
3. Deductive

INDEX